# Ginosko

## A Call To Intimacy

Nicholas Mark Kusmich Jr.

Ginosko – A Call to Intimacy
Copyright © 2012
Nicholas Mark Kusmich Jr.

**ALL RIGHTS RESERVED**
No portion of this publication may be reproduced, stored in any electronic system, or transmitted in any form or by any means, electronic, mechanical, photocopy, recording, or otherwise, without written permission from the author. Brief quotations may be used in literary reviews.

Cover art by Rivonny Luchas. *www.vonluchas.com*
Cover Image by Bent Fork 2008

All Scripture quotations, unless otherwise indicated are taken from the Holy Bible. New King James Version

ISBN-13: 978-1477458976
ISBN-10: 1477458972

**FOR INFORMATION, CONTACT:**
Please visit our websites at:
    www.SOZOCommission.com
    www.EQUIPAcademy.com

# ACKNOWLEDGEMENTS

A millions thanks to:

Dad. I miss you tons! Always trying to make you proud.

Mom. You are the absolute best. I am who I am because of you. I love you.

Steve and Elisa Lee. For demanding that I write something and sending me to LA for a week to do it. This is just the first of many. Thanks for the 'boost'.

Eric and Irma Soetikno. For giving me a place to crash for that week, and taking me around while in LA. I still can't believe you made me eat cow tongue without telling me!

Pasadena House of Prayer and Starbucks in Pasadena. For giving me the venue to sit all day and write.

Isabelle Allum. For the prophetic word over my life reminding me that now is the time to write.

Pastor Anthony Does. For letting me intern under you and always giving me opportunities to minister. This book is the result of my prayer time at the back of the bus during Go Canada '99. Awesome trip.

Trevor Vanier. For giving me my first shot as a pastor and believing in me all the way

Peter Karl Youngren. For being one of the few people I can be totally honest with all the time and for all the support at every crossroad in my life.

Mark Virkler. For opening up my eyes to a whole new understanding of Christianity.

My Immanuel family. For giving me a place to share my thoughts every Sunday. And for all the love and support. How can I ever show my thanks?!

To all my friends and family. For always being behind me in good times and bad. I don't know where I'd be without you.

Von Luchas. Thank you for all your support and masterful work. You are a creative genius.

Bonita Jewel, editor extraordinaire. This wouldn't have been possible without you. Thanks for always going over and above for me. You're the best!

Soraya. A thousand thanks with love.

# Table of Contents

Introduction: Was This Christianity?...................1

CHAPTER 1: You Ain't Seen Nothing Yet......................5

CHAPTER 2: Then He Spoke..........................................17

CHAPTER 3: What Have We Done with Jesus? ..........27

CHAPTER 4: The Realities of Love................................33

CHAPTER 5: Love? ........................................................41

CHAPTER 6: The Real Definition of Love ....................51

CHAPTER 7: ABBA.........................................................81

CHAPTER 8: Distorted Father Images ......................101

CHAPTER 9: Prodigal God ..........................................115

CHAPTER 10: Daddy Loves You.................................129

CHAPTER 11: Knowing and Believing.......................153

CHAPTER 12: What now?............................................177

Endnotes ........................................................................197

# Was This Christianity?

Many years ago, about four months after I had "become a Christian," I was attending a "revival" meeting that was being hosted by a friend's church. They had brought in a special guest speaker from out of town who was well known for his ministry.

I remember it being a vibrant church—loud and upbeat music, people dancing during praise and worship; the preaching was loud, engaging and exciting.

Towards the end of the sermon the speaker asked the music team to come up and join him, and—almost as if it was planned and rehearsed—they started to play some slow, moving music.

The speaker spoke in a slow, calm voice, and asked us to all bow our heads and close our eyes to go before the Lord in prayer.

After some words, and while the music continued to play, he asked if anyone in the room wanted to become a Christian. He said that if people would simply repeat a prayer after him, they could become a Christian right there in their seats. He said that if they repeated that prayer after him, they could be sure that after they died, they would go to Heaven and not hell.

He started praying, one line at a time, leaving time and space after each sentence for anyone who wanted to repeat the prayers. After he was done, he said, "Now, with every head bowed, and every eye closed, if you prayed that prayer for the first time and accepted Jesus into your heart, raise your hand so I can know and continue praying for you." He mentioned that nobody would be looking but him, so to raise their hands and acknowledge that they had just given their life to the Lord.

Then the speaker started to say, "I see that hand over there, thank you. I see a hand in the back. I see some young women in the front . . . " He proceeded to acknowledge all the hands that were going up all over the room.

During this entire time, as I was sitting in the very back pew of the church, I had kept my eyes open and was watching the whole thing take place.

*I didn't see a single hand go up . . .*

Really?

Was this what Christianity was all about?

And even if people did put their hands up and had prayed that prayer, was it that simple? Was that all it took?

Repeat a prayer and you're "good"?

*Introduction: Was This Christianity?*

And what of all the people who prayed that kind of prayer and just went back to living the same old life the very next day?

None of this was sitting well with me.
I was unsettled about the fact that he was lying about the hands going up.

I was unsettled about the fact that a simple prayer (no matter what you did with your life after that prayer) was all it took to be a "Christian."

None of this was sitting well with me.

Surely, God and Christianity was more than this.

Was this all that God wanted from us?
This couldn't be all that it was.

But if this wasn't "it", then *what was*?

## CHAPTER 1

# You Ain't Seen Nothing Yet

I remember it like it was yesterday. As I stood on a hillside, the most beautiful elements of nature filled the scene behind me — two snow-peaked mountains, large green trees and an emerald lake all served as a magical backdrop.

It's arguably Canada's most beautiful piece of land – Banff Lake Louise National Park. And it truly was beautiful. I have traveled the world and seen a lot of beautiful places, but this spot was a gem.

The sun was warm, and only a few faint voices could be heard in the distance – tourists admiring the scenery.

In front of me, a group of over twenty young people eagerly waited to hear what I had to share. We had just finished singing some worship songs, and God's presence was keenly felt. Maybe it was just the majestic scenery behind, or perhaps something else was going on, but I knew at that moment that the ground I was standing on was holy. I had come a long way from that evening at the "revival" and I knew that my journey was only just beginning.

That morning, surrounded by peace and beauty, it was almost as though I didn't even need to say anything. With the picturesque background—a perfect representation of God's majestic creation—and the beautiful presence, we all felt the touch of His hand. It was almost as if all I had to say was "God" and that would be sufficient.

But it was my turn to share the "devotional" and what came out of my mouth that sunny afternoon not only became the foundation of this book you are holding in your hand, but it also radically changed my life and set the course of my ministry.

But to understand how we got to that point, I'll need to rewind and take you back several years.

## A Deal like Hannah's

I am an only child. In fact, my very conception was a miracle of God. My mother was barren. She and my father had tried for years to have children but with no success. After much frustration and despair—as many women face who are trying to have children go through—she, like Hannah in the Bible, made a "deal" with God [1 Samuel Chapter 1]. Although my mother was not a Christian at the time, she threw up a desperate prayer that any want-to-be mom would pray: "God, if You are out there and You give me a child, You can then use him for whatever You want in life."

## Chapter 1: You Ain't Seen Nothing Yet

Without really knowing what she did, maybe not even believing it totally, she was setting in motion a miraculous series of events that would change her life and the lives of so many others.

Not too long after this, her friend introduced her to a Pentecostal woman pastor who mom's friend said could possibly help her out by praying for her. My mom agreed and this pastor laid hands on her, praying for a child.

That same month, she conceived me.

She also became a believer and her experience with this new "mysterious" God, who just answered her heart's cry, began.

From my early childhood, I could "feel" a sense of destiny. I could tell something was a little different, although I could never put my finger on it.

When I was in the sixth grade, my mother was attending a church service that had a special guest speaker from out of town. After his message, as he was going around the room praying for and ministering to people, he stopped my mother as she was actually on her way out of the room, and he gave her a "word."

The first word was something very specific with regards to her marriage (that probably saved her marriage). Then he said to her: "You have an only son. A son who was not supposed to be born." Amongst several other things, which in fact did come to pass later in my life, he said, "He is called into the ministry and the Lord has set him apart for a great task."

I remember the day she came home and told me that story. I started to laugh. "Ministry? Ya right! So I can be stressed and poor my whole life? No thanks!"

She then tried to explain and make me feel better by saying, "It just means you are going to do good work for the Lord in whatever you do."

I again laughed and said, "We'll see."

## Just Like Jonah

A couple of years after that I started attending junior high in a brand new school district[1]. I remember the first day of school was actually frightening. I had been in the same school my whole life up to this point[2]. I had always kept all the same friends and was in my own little comfort zone. I had been popular, school president, liked by many people and many teachers through my elementary years; now I found myself in brand new school where I didn't know a single person.

I remember walking into the auditorium for orientation and everyone had their little groups of friends. I tried to scan the room to see if there was anyone sitting alone with whom I could try to make friends, but it felt like I was the only new guy.

Then some big, rough guy who was sitting with a group of other tough-looking people called me over and told me to sit with them. I was relieved yet worried, thankful yet anxious at the same time.

I was thankful that a group was open and willing to take me in. But if I were to judge a book by its cover, then this "story" didn't look like it was going to be one full of flowers and rainbows.

They say (whoever they are)[3], "Show me your friends, and I'll tell you the kind of person you are." Well, within a month or so I

Chapter 1: You Ain't Seen Nothing Yet    9

found myself caught up in a bunch of stuff that I never imagined that I'd be doing. I'll spare you the details, but very quickly I had built a reputation of not being the nicest guy around.

Deep down I knew it was wrong, and even these guys would admit something was different about me . . . but at the same time I didn't want to change.

I felt like I was a Jonah, running away from the calling that God had for me. Although I wasn't swallowed up by a big fish, I was swallowed up by the "world"–the lust of the eyes, the lust of the flesh and the pride of life.

It was then that I realized that no matter how fast or how far you run, you cannot outrun this wonderful and beautiful God.

He pursued me relentlessly. No matter what I was doing, I could feel Him there in everything, even the "bad" things. I could sense His presence, even though I didn't know what that meant; there was a tugging of my heart that I just couldn't shake.

## My Salvation - Walking in the Calling

The summer after I graduated Junior High, I attended a Summer Youth Retreat with my church[4]. By this point I had gotten really good at living a double life. I was the "president" of my youth group and a spiritual leader at church on Sunday and mid-week service. Every other day of the week I was the opposite: singing songs of love to Jesus one day, smoking pot and beating people up the next. I had become a pure poser who had successfully learned how to "play the game" of Christianity.

I knew when to say, "Amen." I knew when to raise my hands

during a worship song (everyone knows you raise your hands during the chorus), and I had learned how to pray with big Biblical words that would impress the hearers.

I was one of those guys who the prophet was talking about when he said, "They honor me with their lips, but their hearts are far from me" (Isaiah 29:13, Matthew 15:8, Mark 7:6). I was a hypocrite to the core!

That evening, we had just finished dinner and I went to the chapel area to help prepare for our evening service.
I was alone in the room, setting up sound equipment, when I heard the voice of God. I don't know if it was audibly but it sure sounded like it to me.

He said, "Nick, you have been running away too long. I love you too much to allow you to keep running. I have a great plan for you. It's time to start walking in your calling."

Once I got over the initial shock and awe of what was happening, I responded, "Lord, I know, but if I am going to do this Christianity and ministry thing, it's got to be different. I am not happy with what I see and it doesn't sit well in my heart. Surely You are bigger and better than what has been presented to me as 'Christianity' and 'Ministry'."

Although I couldn't physically see Him, I sensed He was smiling and saying, "You ain't seen anything yet! What I have in store for you and the church cannot be fathomed with your natural mind. I will show you along the way. Just walk with Me, and I promise a journey you'll never forget—full of adventure."

And just like that — without any special music, a run down to the altar, someone leading me in prayer, thunder and lightening — I

## Chapter 1: You Ain't Seen Nothing Yet

had my own salvation experience.

That night in the service—without anyone knowing what had happened to me earlier—something inside me changed.

The guest pastor[5] prayed for me and I "fell out under the power." I didn't "come to" until the next day. I was told they carried me into the bedroom and put me on the bed where I found myself the next morning.

During the time I was "out," I had dreams (or visions) about all that I would be doing in life and ministry. Some were clear, vivid, full-color blueprints—what my ministry would be like, the countries I would reach, and the stages on which I would stand and share His message. Others were only glimpses, places where I felt God was telling me that I could "fill in the blanks".

I started to recognize the gifts God had given me, and how they complemented these visions. It was a wild experience that changed my life.

It was the beginning of a journey that could truly only be described as, "you ain't seen anything yet."

## From Detention to Destiny

A few weeks later I started my tenth grade year, in a new high school[6]. Fresh off this God experience, I really didn't know what to expect.

Could I stay true to the calling of God on my life?
Would I meet new people who would open new doors for me?

Although my behavior and conduct had changed instantly after my experience (I no longer smoked pot and beat people up), I didn't know how else my life would change.

On the first day of school I remember vaguely hearing on the announcements something about "Missing Peace Christian Fellowship" meeting after school, but I didn't catch where it was going to be held. I felt like it was something I wanted to be a part of but wasn't sure how to go about it, having missed the details.

My last period class was geography—held outside in a portable classroom. My teacher[7] was a little annoyed that I was talking during class and I ended up with a detention. I had to stay back after class for 30 minutes—bummer! Not a good start to the year. The final bell rang and everyone left the class except me. I sat there reading a book, counting the seconds to pass until I could finally go home.

I looked up when I noticed people starting to walk into the portable. A couple of them carried guitars. I figured it was just other people who had gotten detentions from other classes. More and more people came in and, before I had time to figure out what was going on, they started singing praise and worship songs! It was the Christian fellowship!–Missing Peace. God had used my big mouth for my good (something that truly only God can do).

I met some wonderful people over the next several weeks through Missing Peace, including one girl who invited me to her church's Wednesday night Youth Service—Toronto Youth On Fire. I attended and I loved it! I had never seen a youth service like this before—150 or so young people, loud music, lights blaring everywhere, and people just loving God and each other.

I had found my home. Over the next several months, through what can only be described as God's set-ups, I was interning under the youth pastor[8] and learning more than I ever had before. I had begun taking steps towards my destiny.

## From Coast to Coast with the Holy Ghost

The youth pastor then handed me my first major assignment: plan a nationwide mission trip/tour taking a group of young people across Canada, to pray 24/7 and hold revival services in every major city of the country. Our motto was "coast to coast with the Holy Ghost" . . . and I had about ten months to plan it. Talk about getting the most out of your interns!

After those months, filled with preparation, stress and hard work, a group of twenty-two youth, six adults and our pastor set off by plane from Toronto to St John's, Newfoundland (the most eastern point in North America), to start our journey.

We dipped our feet in the Atlantic Ocean and then started our trip, knowing that approximately twenty-eight days later we would be dipping our feet in the Pacific, having completed our prayer and revival service adventure.

One mission of the tour was to be praying twenty-four hours a day; we would assign one person in one- to two-hour rotations to pray around the clock.

Along with this, every member of the team was scheduled to share a devotional on what the Lord was revealing to him or her during his or her prayer time.
It was incredible.

The insights and revelations that the young people were receiving from Heaven were simply amazing.

Before we even held our first service, as we flew from Toronto to St. Johns, Newfoundland, one of the girls[9] was praying. She shared with us that she saw waves of fire rolling over the service that we were en route to minister in.

We arrived and started the service. After some rousing praise and worship, our pastor stepped up to share the message. As he was preaching, he turned to look out the window and then dropped his microphone. We all stopped to follow his gaze outside and this was what we saw.

The clouds had formed what looked like waves and although you can't tell from this picture, the colors were a vibrant red and orange with hints of blue and purple. "Waves of fire!"

As we began to minister that night, the power of God was tangible in the room as healings, miracles, and deliverances began to take place with so many people.
The awesome night didn't end until after 1:30am. Some of the congregation members invited us to stay with them that night,

since it was so late.

As a few of us packed up, we realized that we were starving; we hadn't eaten since dinner. We started to pray in tongues, jokingly throwing in the word "lasagna" amidst our prayer. (I know, not very reverent, but cut us some slack. We were just teens.) We didn't think anything of it until we arrived at the family's house and there on the table, at two in the morning, was a freshly baked dish of lasagna[10].

God does work in mysterious ways.

CHAPTER 2

# Then He Spoke

We were on the bus, about two-thirds of the trip completed, and the next day I was slotted to share the devotional. The problem was, I had nothing to share (except maybe that lasagna thing, but nothing of real substance).

The best I could come up with was "God loves you" (with a big smile on my face, of course). Not only did I have nothing, but the guy[11] who shared that very morning had this crazy, extravagant revelation about Nebuchadnezzar's vision of the statue (Daniel Chapter 2). Everyone was totally blown away.

So not only did I feel the pressure for not having anything worth sharing, but I was also going up after this profound revelation that had everyone completely astonished.

I went to the back of the bus to pray, as it was my allotted time. Rather than praying for the nation of Canada, I was begging God for some deep revelation that I could share during my devotional time with the others.

## The Vision

After about ten minutes of silence—I don't know if I fell asleep or what exactly happened—I sensed a terrible stench come in through my nostrils. At first I thought it was from the washroom, as the toilet was situated at the back of the bus beside where I sat.

I opened my eyes to find that I was no longer on the bus. I could hear screams of people in torment. The smell was that of sulfur.

Everywhere I looked, people were in agony.
I can only describe what I saw as "hellish."

I thought to myself, *Have I died and gone to hell?*
*What is going on here?*
*Is this just a bad dream?*

I tried to pinch myself to wake up but it wasn't working.

I then started to notice that I could recognize some of the people who were there with me. People who I had gone to school with. Even people I currently went to church with. I was frightened and confused.

I cried out to God for help. I asked Him to make this all stop. I couldn't stand it anymore.

I then heard His voice.

"People are living in agony and torment because they don't know the truth. Tell them the truth, and the truth shall set them free" (John 8:32).

I said "I will, Lord. I will tell them whatever you want me to tell them." I then "woke up" out of the experience and realized that I was still in the back of the bus.

## John 3:16

I felt the Lord encourage me to start reading the book of John. I got through the first two chapters and into the third when I came across the most famous and widely known passage in the whole Bible—the famous John 3:16.

I breezed through it:

> *For God so loved the world that He gave His only begotten Son, that whoever believes in Him should not perish but have everlasting life.*

And as I continued to read, I heard Him say to me, "Stop! Read it again."

I read it again:

> *For God so loved the world that He gave His only begotten Son, that whoever believes in Him should not perish but have everlasting life.*

As I went on reading, He said once more,

"Stop! Read it again."

I said, "Lord, I don't need to read it again. I memorized this verse. It is a verse that I, and probably almost everyone else in the world, knows.

'For God so loved the world that He gave his only begotten son that whosoever believes in Him should not perish but have everlasting life.'"

He asked me, "Did you see it?"

"See what?"

"Read it one more time." He said.

"Really???

> For God so loved the world that He gave His only begotten Son, that whoever believes in Him SHOULD NOT perish... (Emphasis added.)

And then I saw it.

I had always read that as *"shall not"* but it didn't say that.
It said, *"should not."*[12]
*Shall* and *should* are different words . . . very different.

For example, if you were to study very hard for a test, you should not fail, but you still could.

If you were to practice lots at hitting the baseball, you should not strike out, but you still might.

"For God so loved the world that He gave His only begotten Son that whosoever believes in Him should not perish". . . but could.

## Chapter 2: Then He Spoke

"Wait a second, God! This messes up everything I ever believed to be true about Christianity. I thought if I just believe, I will have eternal life."

"Yes it's true, that if one believes in Christ they *should* not perish of course, but they *could*."

"How, Lord?"
"You're going to have to show me more."

James says that even the demons believe and shutter [James 2:19].

"So then what is eternal life? How can we get it?"

And the Lord told me to keep reading the book of John.

I did and I came across the seventeenth chapter. Three verses in, I read, "And this is eternal life," (John 17:3).

Bingo! John comes out clearly here and is about to tell us what eternal life is. Whatever comes after this comma is the answer to what I was seeking.

> *And this is eternal life, that they may <u>know</u> You, the only true God, and Jesus Christ whom You have sent.*

Eternal life is about "knowing" God?

What does this mean?

I looked up the world "know" and found that it comes from the Greek word *ginosko*.
I also discovered that it is one of the most "personal" verbs in the Greek language.

*Ginosko* means:
- to intimately know, feel
- to become known
- to understand

It is also an intimate term and was a Jewish idiom for sexual intercourse between a man and a woman.

The Hebrew equivalent is *yada,* a word used in Genesis 4 when it says, "And Adam *knew* Eve his wife; and she conceived . . . "

Eternal life is coming to intimately know God.

I then realized it wasn't about:
- Repeating some prayer
- Asking Jesus into my heart
- Becoming a member of a church
- Singing some songs
- Following a bunch of laws, rules, conducts, and codes

I said, "Lord, if this is true, You need to show me more in Your Word."

Thus begun a sort of treasure hunt, as He led me to several other passages that prove the same point.

> *Enter by the narrow gate; for wide is the gate and broad is the way that leads to destruction, and there are many who go in by it (Matt. 7:13).*

> *Not everyone who says to Me, 'Lord, Lord,' shall enter the kingdom of heaven, but he who does the will of My Father in heaven. Many will say to Me in that day, 'Lord, Lord, have we not prophesied in Your name, cast out demons in Your name,*

## Chapter 2: Then He Spoke

> *and done many wonders in Your name?' And then I will declare to them, 'I never <u>knew</u> you; depart from Me, you who practice lawlessness (Matt. 7:21-23).*

He starts by saying we need to be sure to enter by the narrow gate for there are many who go the way of destruction.

He then refers to a time when people are looking to enter the kingdom of Heaven, claiming as their entrance ticket some of the works they did for the kingdom of God.

And look at His response.
"I never knew ("ginosko'd") you. Depart from me."

In others words, "Yes you may have done all these things, but you didn't intimately know Me. You didn't have a personal relationship with Me. We weren't intimately acquainted."

A similar passage in Luke states the same thing.

> *Strive to enter through the narrow gate, for many, I say to you, will seek to enter and will not be able. When once the Master of the house has risen up and shut the door, and you begin to stand outside and knock at the door, saying, "Lord, Lord, open for us," and He will answer and say to you, "I do not <u>know</u> you, where you are from," then you will begin to say, "We ate and drank in Your presence, and You taught in our streets." But He will say, "I tell you I do not <u>know</u> you, where you are from. Depart from Me, all you workers of iniquity"*
> *(Luke 13:24-27).*

He starts again by saying, "strive." Another translation says, "Make every effort" to enter through this narrow gate, for many are going to try to get in, and will not be able to.

Again, it gives us a picture of people who expected to be able to "get in" because of their associations or actions, yet they find a similar answer:

> *"I do not know you."*

Modern vernacular might read,
"But Lord, I . . .
   Attended church almost regularly (mostly on time)
   Read my Bible every so often
   Sang worship songs
   Went to prayer meetings, home cell groups, and revival services."

Yes, but did we really *know* (ginosko) God?

I soon came across the commonly known parable about the ten virgins in Mathew 25. You are probably familiar with the story.

Ten virgins are waiting to meet their bridegroom. The writer tells us that five were wise and five were not so wise. The Bible uses the term "foolish."

He describes the foolish ones as those who had lamps but didn't take enough oil to carry them through the night; the wise ones had enough oil for their lamps.

The story tells us that the foolish ones then had to go out and get oil for their lamps, which had gone out.

Let's pick up the story from there.

> *And while they went to buy, the bridegroom came, and those who were ready went in with him to the wedding; and the door was shut. Afterward the other virgins came also, saying, "Lord, Lord,*

## Chapter 2: Then He Spoke

> *open to us!" But he answered and said, "Assuredly, I say to you, I do not <u>know</u> you"* (Matt. 25:10-12 Emphasis added).

Once more, the similar response – "I do not know you."

This parable has potentially different ramifications, depending on your interpretations of it.

Here is one possibility . . .

We are taught scripturally that the bridegroom is Jesus and the virgins (the bride of Christ) represent the church [Revelation 19:7, 21:2, 9-10].

If this parable is prophetic (which a fair number of people believe it is), this could be implying that fifty percent of the church is not prepared for the return of the bridegroom.

Fifty percent of the "church" does not "know" God.

How true is that in the Christian world?
How many are just "playing" church?
How many people are just going through the motions of being a Christian without ever intimately knowing God?

How much of what we have is just religious activity versus intimate, experiential relationship?

And what does that really mean for us?

How many relationships do you know that has the ability to thrive on mere lip service and empty actions rather than passionate, love sharing?

Could it be that the God of the universe is actually interested in intimacy with His creation, His children?

Could it be that He prefers this to robotic, religious people who follow a set of rules, laws and codes that somehow label us as a certain faith group?

I would argue that not only does the Father desire intimacy (and our true heart's cry is intimacy with our Father) but that this is what eternal life is really all about. It is what Christ came to restore.

You see, "this" –
    life,
    Christianity,
    our faith
is all about intimacy.

The Father's heart is intimacy with His children.

CHAPTER 3

# What Have We Done with Jesus?

Somehow, someway, somewhere, the vibrant spirit and life of Christianity has been lost, buried beneath a bunch of rules or codes that have been given the label of "Christianity."

Many feel that by attending a regular church service, they are in some way a Christian. I heard someone say that sitting in church doesn't make you a Christian any more than standing in a garage makes you a car.

Some feel that if they fulfill "Christian" duties—like reading their Bible, attending home study groups, singing during the worship portion of the service or fasting regularly—they are meeting their obligation of being Christian.

Others believe that as long as they follow a specific moral code—treating others with kindness, giving to worthy causes, living a life that is respectable in the eyes of most—then they will be granted eternal life.

Still others believe that if you just "accept Jesus into your heart," you are "saved." That by praying a prayer at one point in your life gives you the magic stamp of approval into the Kingdom of God. Nowhere in the Bible will we find the instruction or encouragement to accept Jesus into our heart by repeating some sort of prayer.

This is not to say that these things are wrong or bad, but if these are *all* that we look at and use to classify ourselves as Christians, perhaps we need to take a second look at things.

## The Super Christian

I am personally an achiever. Once I set my heart on something, I like to do it, and do it well. My attitude is that if you don't do something with excellence and with all your heart and might, it's not worth doing.

As a result, much of my "faith" was based on what I did. Not long after my salvation experience, I began to attend church more and more frequently.

> Sunday service
> Wednesday night mid-week service
> Friday prayer meeting
> A special service at least once a week

I would be the first to arrive and the last to leave.

## Chapter 3: What Have We Done with Jesus?

I started fasting every lunch in high school, and spent that time sitting in the library reading my Bible and praying.

I was involved in every kind of ministry I could think of at church - worship, ushering, theatrical arts, prayer. I was literally doing some form of church activity six to seven days a week. Every week.

I was a "super Christian" and took great pride in it. I was serving God well, and found value in my performance for Him.

Although I was doing all this, I still felt empty. It was like the more I did, the emptier I felt.

Not only that, but I would grow angry with other Christians who wouldn't do as much as me but somehow seemed to have much more joy than me. I was your classic Martha while being upset with the "Mary's" in my life.[13]

I knew how to pretend that everything was ok and say all the right words on the outside. But inside I was empty.

Even after God spoke to me, even after receiving salvation, even after beginning to fulfill the plan I knew He had for me, something was still missing.

I was stressed.
I was unhappy.
I was unfulfilled.

How could this be? I was doing all the "right" things.

The problem was that I didn't *know* God.

## The Heartbeat of God is a Call to Intimacy

Do we know God? More importantly, does He know us?

This lack of true intimacy is the reason why so many people who call themselves Christians—just like I did—despite how much they do (or don't do) still never find true fulfillment in God.

The longing in their heart remains an empty void.

Part of that is because they think Christianity is based on a bunch of "things" that we need to do.

It's almost as though we label Christians more based on what they do and don't do (they don't smoke or drink alcohol; they attend church and read their Bible) rather than *who they really are*.

Most Christians I talk to are tired and always feel like they are letting God down because they are not living "right."

It's like they have a to-do list for Christianity:
    Wake up and spend an hour in prayer
    Spend another hour reading and studying the Bible
    Be sure to always ask "What Would Jesus Do" before doing anything
    Pray before your meals
    Attend church every Sunday
    Tithe regularly
And the list goes on and on.

It is not that any of these activities are wrong in themselves. Many of them are a healthy part of a Christian lifestyle. Yet so often, Christians feel that if they don't do this, or if they miss one of them, they have let God down and are not living up to the

### Chapter 3: What Have We Done with Jesus?

standard of Christianity. It's a vicious cycle of accomplishment, failure and condemnation.

How can *anyone* live like that and still have a fulfilling and joyful life?

Is that what God desires?

Is there another, better way?

***

I was watching a show called "The Hour."[14] It's a show where the host interviews several media-worthy individuals about what they are currently doing that is making the news.

The guest that particular day was A. J. Jacobs[15], a young Jewish man from Manhattan. He had a long, dirty-looking beard and wore what looked like simple Mormon clothing. In the show, he was describing to the host his latest experiment, which he called "A Year of Living Biblically." He spent a year attempting to follow the innumerous laws contained in the Old Testament Scripture.

He let his beard grow, wore only garments made of unmixed fibers, prayed regularly, essayed biblical disciplining (short of the physical) of his two-year-old son, and practiced the purity laws: no sex for seven days after his wife menstruated, no shaking hands, lots of washing, not eating "unclean" foods, et cetera, *ad infinitum*, it seems.

I don't know if his goal was to find God, or to prove a point with this "experiment".

Regardless, is this what God desires of us?

Is that what He really wants?

Obviously not.

It's not even like we could do this. Even if we could, I would bet that it would not bring fulfillment.

I knew it didn't work for me.

If we were honest with ourselves and looked at our innermost parts, I think many of us would agree that something is still missing.

Something doesn't feel complete.

It's not all there.

There is still a void . . .

A void that can only be filled by intimacy with our Creator.

## Chapter 4

# The Realities of Love

Do you remember the first time you watched the movie *The Passion of the Christ*?

I do. It was with my church. We had rented out the whole theatre just for our church to watch the film. It was very moving. There were certain parts of the movie I almost couldn't get through.

You probably know which parts I am talking about.

The flogging at the scourging post was one such scene.
Jesus was taken to the scourging post before His crucifixion. For once, a more realistic portrayal of what actually happened.

Maybe you are like me and have seen hundreds of paintings of Jesus nailed to a cross with a little blood trickling from his head, hands and feet. Rarely do you see an image where His body was torn to pieces.

The Roman cat-of-nine-tails whip was a brutal torture instrument made of nine long leather straps with embedded glass, stones and bones in them. This whip was designed to torture an individual. The first-century historian Flavius Josephus noted that certain rebel Jews were torn to pieces by the scourging even before being crucified on the execution pole.[16]

The Roman historian Livy states, "The Romans employed scourging as torture or punishment to extract information."[17]

It should not surprise you to learn that "sometimes the victims died before the scourging was finished. Scourging sometimes led to the death of the condemned person."[18]

"Their bodies were frightfully lacerated. Christian martyrs in Smyrna were so torn by the scourges that their veins were laid bare, and the inner muscles, sinews, even entrails, were exposed."[19] In other words, if the Roman lictors—the two soldiers on either side who took turns whipping the victims—weren't careful, they could cut major veins or disembowel the victim, causing premature death.

It is a common understanding that Jesus was whipped forty—minus one—times. Multiply that by nine because the whip had nine strands. When they were done with Him, you couldn't even recognize Jesus as a human being [Isaiah 52:14].

And as if that weren't enough, He then had to undergo the actual tortuous crucifixion.

Chapter 4: The Realities of Love 35

Dr. Mark Eastman gives his medical perspective of what happened at the crucifixion.

### Crucifixion
*It is arguably the most painful death ever invented by man and is where we get our term "excruciating." It was reserved primarily for the most vicious of criminals.*

*The most common device used for crucifixion was a wooden cross, which consisted of an upright pole permanently fixed in the ground with a removable crossbar, usually weighing between 75-100 lbs. Victims of crucifixion were typically stripped naked and their clothing divided by the Roman guards. In Jesus' case this was done in fulfillment of Psalm 22:18, "They divide My garments among them, and for My clothing they cast lots."*

*As a gesture of "Roman kindness" the prisoner was offered a mixture of vinegar (gall) and wine as a mild anesthetic. This anesthetic was refused by Jesus. Consequently, He bore it all!*

*The Apostle Peter stated of Jesus:*
*Who his own self bare our sins in his own body on the tree, that we, being dead to sins, should live unto righteousness: by whose stripes ye were healed. 1 Peter 2:24*
*The victim was then placed on his back, arms stretched out and nailed to the cross bar. The nails, which were generally about 7-9 inches long, were placed between the bones of the forearm (the radius and ulna) and the small bones of the hands (the carpal bones). (Figure 1.)*

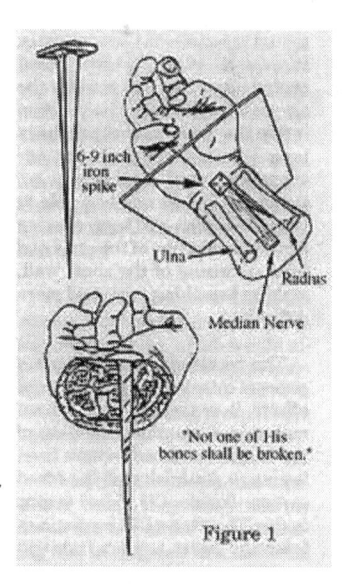

Figure 1

*The placement of the nail at this point had several effects. First it ensured that the victim would indeed hang there until dead. Secondly, a nail placed at this point would sever the largest nerve in the hand called the median nerve.*

*The severing of this nerve is a medical catastrophe. In addition to severe burning pain the destruction of this nerve causes permanent paralysis of the hand. Furthermore, by nailing the victim at this point in the wrist, there would be minimal bleeding and there would be no bones broken! Thus scriptures were fulfilled: I can count all my bones: they look and stare upon me. Psalm 22:17*

*He keepeth all his bones: not one of them is broken. Psalm 34:20*
*The positioning of the feet is probably the most critical part of the mechanics of crucifixion. First the knees were flexed about 45 degrees and the feet were flexed (bent downward) an additional 45 degrees until they were parallel the vertical pole. An iron nail about 7-9 inches long was driven through the feet between the 2nd and 3rd metatarsal bones. In this position the nail would sever the dorsal pedal artery of the foot, but the resultant bleeding would be insufficient to cause death.*

**The Catastrophic Result**
*The resulting position on the cross sets up a horrific sequence of events which results in a slow, painful death. Having been pinned to the cross, the victim now has an impossible position to maintain. (Figure 2)*

Figure 2

Dislocation of the shoulders

The victim's weight causes rapid fatigue of the legs. The weight is transferred to the arms and torso with catastrophic results.

*With the knees flexed at about 45 degrees, the victim must bear his weight with the muscles of the thigh. However, this is an almost impossible task-try to stand with your knees flexed at 45 degrees for 5 minutes. As the strength of the legs gives out, the weight of the body must now be borne by the arms and shoulders. The result is that within a few minutes of being placed on the cross, the shoulders will become dislocated. Minutes later the elbows and wrists become dislocated. The result of these dislocations is the arms would be as much as seven inches longer than normal.*

*With the arms dislocated, considerable body weight is transferred to the chest, causing the rib cage to be elevated in a state of perpetual inhalation. Consequently, in order to exhale the victim must push down on his feet to allow the rib muscles to relax. The problem is that the victim cannot push very long because the legs are extremely fatigued. As time goes on, the victim is less and less able to bear weight on the legs, causing further dislocation of the arms and further raising of the chest wall, making breathing more and more difficult.*

*The result of this process is a series of catastrophic physiological effects. Because the victim cannot maintain adequate ventilation of the lungs, the blood oxygen level begins to diminish and the blood carbon dioxide ($CO_2$) level begins to rise. This rising $CO_2$ level stimulates the heart to beat faster in order to increase the delivery of oxygen and the removal of $CO_2$.*

*However, due to the pinning of the victim and the limitations of oxygen delivery, the victim cannot deliver more oxygen and the rising heart rate only increases oxygen demand. So this process sets up a vicious cycle of increasing oxygen demand-which cannot be met-followed by an ever increasing heart rate. After several hours the heart begins to fail, the lungs collapse and fill up with fluid, which further decreases oxygen delivery to the tissues. The blood loss and hyperventilation combines to cause severe dehydration. That's why Jesus said, "I thirst." (John 19:28)*

*Over a period of several hours the combination of collapsing lungs, a failing heart, dehydration, and the inability to get adequate oxygen supplies to the tissues cause the eventual death of the victim. The victim, in effect, cannot breath properly and slowly suffocates to death. In cases of severe cardiac stress, such as crucifixion, a victim's heart can even burst. This process is called "Cardiac Rupture." Therefore it could be said that Jesus died of a "broken heart!"*

*To slow the process of death the executioners put a small wooden seat on the cross, which would allow the victim the privilege of bearing his weight on his buttocks. The effect of this was that it could take up to nine days to die on a cross.*

*When the Romans wanted to expedite death they would simply break the legs of the victim, causing him to suffocate in a matter of minutes. At three o'clock in the afternoon Jesus said, "Tetelastai," meaning "it is finished." (John 19:28) Then He gave up the ghost. When the soldiers came to Jesus to break His legs, He was already dead. Not a bone of Him was broken"*[20]

Let's not forget the outright shame that the King of kings was hanging there naked for the whole world to see.

The reason I mention all this is to ask . . .
For what?

Just so we can have pleasant little church services, and sing some nice little songs?

Surely all of what Christ went through was for much more than that.

## Chapter 4: The Realities of Love

Could it be that, with the fall of man, intimacy with the Father was lost, and His heart desired to restore that intimacy regardless of the cost?

Christianity is not just about following a bunch or rules or laws or code of conduct.

It's not about church services with nice songs in nice pews with nice, leather-bound Bibles.

It is about a love relationship with the all-powerful, yet intimately interested, God of the universe.

Have we forgotten what it really means to live?
Have we forgotten our primary purpose in life?
Have we gotten so preoccupied with living life that we have missed really "living life?"

\*\*\*

It had been about a year since that amazing road trip. I was in a worship service, just sitting there enjoying the music as I often did, when in the midst of that I heard the voice of God say to me, "Son, I miss you."

It struck a chord somewhere deep within me. Made me feel a little weird. I thought, "What do You mean, You *miss* me?"

He said: "You serve Me, (and you serve me well) and do all these things for Me (in church ministry and in life), but you are losing your intimacy with Me. I miss you."
I realized that although I was a pastor, I was so busy doing "stuff" that I was losing the essence of who I was and the very thing my heart cried out for–intimacy.

***

It's almost like we have forgotten how to love.

When I was younger, I came across some home videos on those old mini dv tapes. I popped one in and saw a video of my parents at their local convenience store business.

The camera was on me, following me around. I was running away from the camera guy (whoever it was) and was trying desperately to find my dad.

After running up and down the aisles of the store, I finally made it to the back room where my dad's office was.

As soon as I saw him, I ran as fast as I could into his arms.
It's amazing how affectionate children are. We seem to lose that as we grow and "mature."

Is it any wonder that Jesus picks up a child in His arms and says to His disciples, "If you want to anything to do with the Kingdom of God you need to become like one of these" (Matthew 18:3)?

Do you realize that you can go through your whole life . . .
You can go to church for years,
You might even call yourself a Christian, and rightfully so,
. . . yet still not have a real, intimate relationship with God?

The truth is, Christianity without intimacy is not real Christianity. It really is all about Love.

> *"And now abideth faith, hope, love, these three; but the greatest of these is love" (1 Corinthians 13:13).*

# Chapter 5

# Love?

*"Love the Lord your God with all your heart, soul, mind and strength" (Luke 10:27).*

Love.

What an interesting word.
It means so many things to so many people.

I love dogs.
I love hotdogs.
I love the girl I dated back in tenth grade for three months.
And I love God.

Could it all possibly mean the same thing?
Surely not!

Have you ever been in love?
I remember the first time I thought I was in love.

I was in tenth grade.

I liked this girl. In fact, I "loved" her.
We would spend hours talking on the phone.

It didn't always start that way. It was minutes at first. Then a little longer. Then a little longer. Until it was hours.

Sometimes I'd miss dinner because we were talking.

If we were talking late at night, I remember sometimes dozing off and waking up mid-conversation, pretending I never missed a word.

Once, because we didn't want to hang up on each other, I fell asleep with my phone beside the pillow, and she did the same.

Oh, puppy love! Do you remember those days?

Once, it must have been around 2am when we got off the phone. When hanging up, I heard God say to me, "When was the last time you talked to Me all night? You say you love Me and you say you love someone else. If that is what you do for them, what reflects your love for Me?"

I was speechless.

Where WAS my love at?


**When you love someone...**
       **you can't stop talking about them**

## Chapter 5: Love?

Maybe you don't notice it but everyone around you sure does. They're usually too kind to tell you to shut up.

"Last night we went out to eat, and she was so beautiful. She has a little giggle that is so cute!"

You're driving with someone else in the car and stop and a red light and it reminds you of the time you went out with her and she was wearing that red dress, so you go into another whole babble about that night. Your friend finally comes out with, "Dude, enough already!"

When you're in love, you don't have to *force* yourself to talk about that person.

It's not like a husband wakes up thinking, *Ok, today I am going to tell someone about my wife. I think I should pray first, and build some courage.*

And they go into their day and see an acquaintance.

*Oh there is someone, I'll do it right now.*
*No, I won't.*
*Yes. I will.*
*No, I won't.*
*What would they think?*
*I don't think I can do it.*

Sounds a little silly, right?

When you are in love, you don't have to force anything.
It just flows right out.

But then, if we really love the Lord, why is it so hard?
Why is it such a big deal for us to talk about Him?

### When you love someone...
### you spend a lot of money on them

Several years ago, a friend of mine asked if I could help him deliver some roses to his new girlfriend's house for Valentines Day.

I agreed, and when we got to the flower shop, he had bought twelve dozen, red, long-stemmed roses. The Valentines Day pricing made them just over $1200.

People spend crazy money and do crazy things for people they love.

Now if that's true (and it is), why is it that our wallets lock up when it comes to Jesus?

When was the last time we spent some money on Jesus?
I'm not talking about going to the mall and buying Him something.

When we try to do that, it's funny, but everything we buy for Jesus is in our size.

I always say, "It's for the Jesus inside me."

## People do crazy things for love

I am sometimes amazed at how some people proposed to their significant other:

*Chapter 5: Love?* 45

Or my personal favorite:

Imagine the effort involved to pull that one off.

(I think it's funny how the guy in the apartment six stories down from the top in the "I" didn't participate. Maybe it was the exboyfriend.)

But that is extravagant love!

If people would do that for other people, what would the God of the universe do for us?

And what can we be doing for Him?

The purpose for these parallels is to bring this concept into a realm we can readily understand.

Paul says, *"Yet indeed I also count all things loss for the excellence of the knowledge of Christ Jesus my Lord, for whom I have suffered the loss of all things, and count them as rubbish, that I may gain Christ"* (Phil. 3:8).

Paul was a very accomplished person.

Having attended the top school in Tarsus, he had the best education money could afford. He was a chief Pharisee and a respected Roman citizen.

Despite all his accolades, he says that he considers all things as rubbish . . . loss in comparison to the "knowledge" (gnosis) of Christ.

He was saying that the most important thing—the reason for our very existence—is *knowing* God.

And that makes sense, doesn't it.

When you die (and you will eventually), you can't take your car or your clothes, your education or degrees, your job or social status.

All of that will fade away into nothing.

The only thing that will matter at that specific moment is:

*Chapter 5: Love?* 47

Do you know God?
Does He know you?

Paul says again . . .

*"Though I speak with the tongues of men and of angels, but have not love, I have become sounding brass or a clanging cymbal. And though I have the gift of prophecy, and understand all mysteries and all knowledge, and though I have all faith, so that I could remove mountains, but have not love, I am nothing. And though I bestow all my goods to feed the poor, and though I give my body to be burned, but have not love, it profits me nothing"*
*(1 Cor. 13:1-3).*

You can do anything in this world. Anything at all.

You can . . .
   make lots of money
   have a successful business
   be a great musician or artist
   be or do whatever you want

But . . .

If you don't have a relationship with Dad, it is all worthless (all the accomplishments and good deeds).
It profits you nothing.

Because everything revolves around love.

## Seeking the Gift While Forgetting the Giver

A friend of mine told me that when he would come home from

work, his youngest daughter would always drop whatever she was doing and run to the door to greet him with a hug and a kiss. This was her regular practice. It had become a sort of tradition.

One day, after seeing an advertisement for a Barbie, she asked her father if he could get one for her.

Like all good fathers, the next day he came home with a gift for her. As always, his daughter came running to greet him with a hug and a kiss. He gave her the Barbie and she was ecstatic.
The next day was a little different though.

He came home but this time, no pitter-patter of little feet running from the back of the house. He was worried that maybe something happened so he called out to her.

A little voice responded from the back of the house, "I'm here daddy." He rushed to see if everything was alright and there was his daughter . . . playing with her Barbie.

She was so caught up with gift that she forgot the giver.[21]

How often does this happen to us?
We get so caught up in loving the gifts that we forget to love the Giver behind the gifts.

Sometimes this causes us to begin to seek His hands
and not His face.

Let us never forget what life is all about.
Yes, intimacy brings benefits.
But it's never about the benefits.

It's about the love.

## Chapter 5: Love?

If there is one thing that I want to be remembered for on this planet, it wouldn't be all my accomplishments.

I want to be remembered as the guy who *knew* God.

*\*\*\**

Now let me be clear.
There is a difference between knowing *about* God and *knowing* God.

I was told that an expert can look at the paw print of a tiger and, from it, figure out the gender, general age and type of tiger it is.

But there is a big difference between looking at a tiger's paw print and looking a tiger right in the face.

It's once thing to have a good amount of intellectual knowledge about God.

Many non-believing professors who teach the Bible in Universities all over the world have more *knowledge* about God and the Bible than most Christians do.

Does that mean they are walking in intimacy with Him?

Parents can teach their child all about fire. They can explain how it burns and is dangerous.

They can even bring a fireman to come over and teach more about what fire can do and tell stories of how it can be dangerous.

They can even bring in a scientist to talk about all the properties of fire and what it does to human flesh.

But until that child touches the fire, they will only know *about* it.
Without a real experience with fire, it will only be head knowledge.

I invite you today to "touch the fire."
Don't just learn about it.
Don't just memorize details.

Touch It.

## CHAPTER 6

# The Real Definition of Love

So I now knew the message that I was meant to share with the world:

*"Love God with all your heart, soul, mind and strength."*

Everywhere I go, this was the message I would share with the people I interacted with and talked to.

But there was an interesting phenomenon happening. Everywhere I shared this message, people aligned with it. They found it was their heart's cry to be intimate with God. Yet the more they tried to love God, the more they seemed to fail.

Stumbling block after stumbling block, people would come back to me and say:
"I get your message. It makes so much sense. It's what I want.

But how do I love God? Why does it seem so hard? And why does it seem like every time I try, I fail?"

Was *I* missing something?
Was the message incomplete?

I searched my own life and heart and started to realize that I, too, was struggling to love God. It was my heart's deepest desire, but I seemed to keep falling short.

I realized that I had been struggling with this off and on for years.

I continued to tell people to love God with everything they've got. As I observed the effects of my counsel, it seemed like I was putting a greater burden on them rather than setting them free.

Surely this wasn't the way.

He told us that His "yoke is easy" and His "burden is light" (Matt. 11:30).

This "yoke" felt hard and heavy.
Sometimes even condemning.

This couldn't be God's way. We are not to live in condemnation but righteousness, peace and joy in the Holy Ghost.

Where was I going wrong?

Then I found it. Or rather, then He revealed it to me and my eyes were opened.

> "In this the love of God was manifested toward us, that God has sent His only begotten Son into the world, that we might live

## Chapter 6: The Real Definition of Love

*through Him. In this is love, not that we loved God, but that He loved us and sent His Son to be the propitiation for our sins"* (1 John 4:9-10).

The Lord showed me that my problem was in my definition of love. I had it wrong.

Here, John gives us the definition of love.

Most people oftentimes have the wrong definition.

If you were to ask most believers, "What is love?" they will quote the ever-so-famous words of Paul written to the Corinthian people, which are commonly recited at almost every wedding.

*"Love is patient, love is kind. It does not envy, it does not boast, it is not proud. It is not rude, it is not self-seeking, it is not easily angered, it keeps no record of wrongs. Love does not delight in evil but rejoices with the truth. It always protects, always trusts, always hopes, always perseveres. Love never fails"* (1 Corinthians 13:4-8).

Beautiful words indeed.
And much to be learned about love from them.

However, these words are not the *definition* of love but rather the *characteristics* of love. These words are a perfect description of what love looks like in practice.

But through the previous words of John, he actually helps us to define love as it pertains to a person.

*"In this is love, not that we loved God, but that He loved us"* (1 John 4:10).

The essence of love for us in relation to God is all about *God loving us*, over the emphasis of us loving Him.[22]

***

The totality of the Old Testament law,
the entirety of it,
every law and command written in the Hebrew scriptures,
can be summed up in one verse.

In Matthew 22:37-40, Jesus is quoting Deuteronomy and says:

> *"'You shall love the LORD your God with all your heart, with all your soul, and with all your mind.' This is the first and great commandment. And the second is like it: 'You shall love your neighbor as yourself.' On these two commandments hang all the Law and the Prophets."*

Jesus says that according to the Old Testament law, we are to love the Lord our God with all of our heart, soul, mind and strength.

In fact, the entire Old Testament can be summed up in two words:
    Love God.

Not all that hard, is it?

Those chapters full of laws in Leviticus and Deuteronomy, and the Ten Commandments, all seem so confusing.
And there are so many of them.

But Jesus simplified them by saying they are all summed up by loving God.

## Chapter 6: The Real Definition of Love

To keep it even simpler, when you think of the Law (the commandments and rules of the Old Testament), just think of loving God.

It might sound a little weird at first, to associate loving God with the law, but Jesus Himself said it: when you think of the law, think of *you* loving God.

We'll clear that up more in just a second, so stay with me here as we look further at this.

Under the law, man was commanded to love God with everything that he had.

This was the *law*! – A requirement set out by God.

The question is . . . has anyone ever fulfilled it?

Has anyone in this entire world—from the beginning of time until now—ever fulfilled this one simple law, to love God with every single fiber of their being?

Not a chance.

Scripture tells us that the Law wasn't given for us to keep.

It was given to show us how far we have fallen
and to bring us back to Christ [Galatians 3:24].

Loving God is the greatest law of all–the summary of all other laws.

So for fifteen hundred years, man was put under the law to love God, but man could not.

Many people have tried to love God with all that they are, all the time, but have always come short.

Man tried and tried and even the best of them failed.

Even David, a man after God's own heart, could not always live up to this commandment.

I, too, would always tell people to love God!

And they were trying, they really were, but they couldn't seem to do it. Little did I know that I was burdening people with the law and therefore putting people in bondage.

The scriptures tell us that the letter of the law kills and it's a ministry of condemnation and death [2 Corinthians 3:9].

Even though I was telling people to love God—which seemed like the right thing to do—I was making their life and faith that much harder.

## But then comes grace

> *"In this is (true) love (in the New Covenant), not that we loved God, but that He loved us"* (1 John 4:10a).

In God's new way of doing things, the focus is not on our love for God (which, when we tried, didn't work anyway) but rather His love for us.

Under the Old Covenant, God demanded that we love Him with all of our heart, soul, mind and strength.

## Chapter 6: The Real Definition of Love

In the New Covenant, God steps in and says, "Watch me . . I love you with all of my heart," and then He gave His only begotten Son as a propitiation for our sins [1 John 2:2].

This is the emphasis of love — not that we love God, but that He loves us.

And then, as a *result* of this overwhelming and beautiful love that God has for us, we can love Him back.

John tells us later in the passage:
> *"We love Him because He first loved us" (1 John 4:19).*

Are you starting to see this?
So now, the focus is not on our love for God, but on His love for us.

So when you think of the Law, think of *you* loving God.
But when you are realizing Grace, think of *God* loving you.

For example, when Paul writes,
> *"For sin shall not have dominion over you, for you are not under law but under grace" (Romans 6:14).*

. . . you could see it as: "For sin shall not have dominion over you, for you are no longer under the command of you loving God, but under the blessing of God loving you."

The old ways were all about *us*.
  Us obeying commands.
  Us having requirements to meet.
  Us living a certain way.
But the new way is all about God.

  God loving us.

God meeting the righteous requirement of the law on our behalf. God's work on the cross through His Son.

Today and every day, our emphasis, our focus, should not be on how much we love God, but how much He loves us.

## Peter and John

To help you understand this difference and how it affects us in our life—the difference between focusing on our love for Christ versus Christ's love for us—I realized that there are two types of believers.

These believers are often "typed" by Peter and John.

In fact, if you are reading carefully, you will see that all throughout the Gospels, Peter and John are often juxtaposed.

Peter (*Petros* in Greek), whose name means rock or stone, represents the law (as the law was written on stones). And you see how Peter takes pride and boasts in his love for the Lord.

Now remember, whenever your emphasis is on your love for the Lord, whenever you focus on your love for God, you are under the law.

John (Johance), whose name means grace, always had an emphasis and focus in the Lord's love for him.

When you see these two contrasted, you are seeing a contrast of grace—the new ways of doing things where the focus is on Christ—versus the law—the old ways of doing things where the focus is on us.

## The Disciple Whom Jesus Loved

When reading the Gospels, I came across this phrase: "John, the disciple whom Jesus loved."

I always thought this was a little bit strange.

Didn't you?

Was it that John had some sort of characteristic that the others didn't? Or did he know something that caused Jesus to love him more than the others?

Or was it something he did?

I never quite understood it.

Then, when I looked into this further, I realized that this statement: "John, the disciple whom Jesus loved," only appeared in one Gospel–John's!!! (Coincidentally, his Gospel is about love.)

You don't see this statement in Matthew, Mark, or Luke.

Weird, right?
What's this all about?

Did John just have a big head and an inflated ego?
What was John's point in making such a statement?

I think he was practicing what we have been talking about here in this book.

Practicing grace — where he is focusing on *God's* beautiful love *for him*.

Let me illustrate.

Let's say last night, I went out to dinner with three of my pastor friends.

Pastor John
Pastor Mark
Pastor Joe
And myself

When I return home after a great night of wings while watching the game, I write in my journal (I actually don't keep a diary so this is hypothetical).

> *Tonight, four of us went out for some wings and to watch the game. Pastor John, Pastor Mark, Pastor Joe and the Pastor whom Jesus loves.*

I know it sounds a little silly, and you would probably never write this, even if you do keep a diary, but this would not be arrogance. I would just be practicing and emphasizing grace—focusing on the fact that I am the object of God's love and affection.

In fact, I think we all need to do that a little more, lest we forget God's love for us.

Try it with me right now.
Say, "I am the _____ (son or daughter) that Jesus loves."

Feels good to say it, doesn't it?
Knowing that you are so dearly loved.

It's a good practice to include in your life on a regular basis. Every day.

It's not that Jesus loved John any more than He loved the other disciples. He loved them all the same; we all know that. But it was John who really knew it and believed it.

John *focused* on it.

Peter, on the other hand, was the guy who always focused on his love for Jesus.

He is the one who said,
"Lord I love you. Even if all these (referring to the disciples) betray you, I would never, ever, ever betray you" (Matthew 26:33). He was focusing on his love for Christ.

## 5 Lessons to Be Learned

I decided to look up every time this phrase, "the disciple whom Jesus loved," showed up in the Gospel of John to see if there was anything special to learn from it.

This phrase is used five times (the number of grace by the way) and each time, there is a contrast between John and Peter — between someone who focuses on their love for God (Peter – the law) and someone who focuses on God's love for them (John – grace).

It's as though John is trying to prove a point.

Let's take a look at each of these five times.

## #1 – at the Last Supper

> *When Jesus had said these things, He was troubled in spirit, and testified and said, "Most assuredly, I say to you, one of you will betray Me." Then the disciples looked at one another, perplexed about whom He spoke. Now there was leaning on Jesus' bosom one of His disciples, whom Jesus loved. (John 13:21-26)*

This narrative takes place at what is commonly known as the Last Supper. (You know the famous Da Vinci painting?)

Jesus and His disciples are gathered around a table having the Passover dinner.

Now Hebrew culture would show us that they were probably sitting on the floor with a low table where the food would be placed.

The disciples are all sitting around this table, and John (the disciples whom Jesus loved) is sitting beside Jesus, actually leaning on His chest.

At some point during dinner, Jesus states that someone there is going to betray Him and all the disciples are perplexed about whom He was talking about.

The narrative continues:
> *Simon Peter therefore motioned to him (John) to ask who it was of whom He spoke. Then, leaning back on Jesus' breast, he said to Him, "Lord, who is it?"*
>
> *Jesus answered to him (John), "It is he to whom I shall give a piece of bread when I have dipped it." And having dipped the bread, He gave it to Judas Iscariot, the son of Simon.*

## Chapter 6: The Real Definition of Love

Let's notice some apparent differences.

First, John had intimacy.
He seemed to be closer to Jesus than the others.
He was the only disciple leaning on Jesus' chest.

You could almost sense that he really did love the Lord and knew how much the Lord loved him.

Intimacy is usually a shared experience.
But I want you to notice something else here about the narrative that is revealed.

John's intimacy led to knowing "secrets."

Jesus says, "Someone is going to betray me . . . "

Peter (the one who focuses on his love for the Lord), rather than asking Jesus himself (for whatever reason; I can only assume it was because of a lack of intimacy), motioned to John (the one who focuses on Christ's love for him) and asked him who Jesus was speaking off (assuming that John, the one who was close to the Lord, knew or could easily find out).

John obviously didn't know, but watch what he does . . .

> *Then, leaning back on Jesus' breast, he said to Him, "Lord, who is it?" Jesus answered, "It is he to whom I shall give a piece of bread when I have dipped it.*

Notice that Jesus answered only John here, not everyone.
It was only John in this particular story who knew who it was that was going to betray Jesus.

When you focus on your love for God, you lack intimacy and

don't know the deeper "secrets" of God.

Focusing on your love for God will always bring a sense of distance between you and God, because you're always trying to love Him. And when you are trying to love God, it always feels like what you have done is not enough.

Have you ever felt like that?

Like no matter what you do, it never seems like enough?

You pray, you read more of your Bible, you do what you can, but it just never feels like it's enough. It always feels like there is a distance between you and God and approaching the throne boldly is not something you have the faith to do.

However, when you focus on God's love for you, you experience divine intimacy, which leads to knowing the deeper things of God.

Your eyes are off your imperfect love and instead on His perfect love. As a result, you are not looking at all your inadequacies and how you fall short—which of course would make you feel the need to keep your distance from a perfect God.

When you gaze at His perfection, His righteousness and His love, you are drawn to intimacy. And as you are drawn into His intimacy, He begins to reveals to you the deeper things of the Kingdom.

We naturally only share our personal, intimate things with people we truly know and trust.

There are details in my life that only a handful of people will ever know. My deepest desires, struggles, longings and certain personal details of my life are reserved only for my closest friends.

## #2 – The Crucifixion

The second time this phrase comes up is when Jesus hanging on the cross.

> *Now there stood by the cross of Jesus His mother, and His mother's sister, Mary the wife of Clopas, and Mary Magdalene. When Jesus therefore saw His mother, and the disciple whom He loved standing by, He said to His mother, "Woman, behold your son!" Then He said to the disciple, "Behold your mother!" And from that hour that disciple took her to his own home. (John 19:25-27)*

Jesus, in His deepest agony, looks down from the cross and He sees four women—His mother, His aunt, the wife of Clopas, and Mary Magdalene—and John.

John (the one who knew Christ's love for him) was the only disciple who remained with Jesus until the very end. In the midst of Jesus' darkest hour, all the other disciples fled while John was making himself available to Christ.

And because of this divine intimacy, he got a "special assignment."

John was trusted with things important to Jesus—His very family- in this case His mother.

That's not to say that certain assignments are more important than others. Each task given us by Jesus is important. Jesus is looking for people He can trust with His work and His people. God will never put His children or bride in harm's way.

It's one thing for me to ask someone to mow my lawn or wash my car. It would something totally different to ask someone to take care for my mother in my absence, especially if my absence were to be permanent. There are only a few people I could or would trust with such a task. And those people are ones I know very well and trust wholeheartedly.

Peter (the one who focused on his love for Christ), who said, "I will never, ever, ever leave or betray you, Jesus," was nowhere to be found.

In fact, not only was he nowhere to be found, when Christ was on trial and people approached him to ask if he knew Christ, he said, "Nope, I never ever knew Him."

With swearing and cursing, he denied it [Mark 14:66-71].

When you focus on your love for God, you don't really make yourself available for use. Yes, you remain busy *doing* as a way to prove your love for God, but not *available*, which is a completely different thing. When you focus on God's love for you, you are at the foot of the cross and you get special assignments that are close to the Father's heart.

There is something that happens deep in your being when you catch the Father's heart. Your heart starts to break for the things that break His.

I once read about a man who came to his wife, and told her that he didn't love her anymore and was leaving her for his new girlfriend. She was not only devastated and hurt by the whole thing but she was also left with nothing. No place to live, no money to feed her kids . . . nothing.

Another couple in their church who had heard about what happened, and who were very much in touch with the heart of God and how much God loves them, called up the woman and told her to get ready as they were going for a drive somewhere.

They picked her up at the place she was staying.
They asked how she was doing and said how sorry they were for all that had happened.

As they drove around the corner, they pulled into the driveway of a house and turned to the woman. They handed her a set of keys and said, "These are the keys of your brand new house. Would you like a tour?"

\*\*\*

Narayanan Krishnan was a bright, young, award-winning chef with a five-star hotel group, short-listed for an elite job in Switzerland. But a quick family visit home before heading to Europe changed everything.
"I saw a very old man eating his own human waste for food," Krishnan said. "It really hurt me so much. I was literally shocked for a second. After that, I started feeding that man and decided this is what I should do the rest of my lifetime."

Since then he has served more than 1.2 million meals—breakfast, lunch and dinner—to India's homeless and destitute, mostly elderly people abandoned by their families and often abused. [23]

\*\*\*

When you are consumed with the love of the Father, you capture a glimpse of His heart and make yourself available for "special" assignments like the ones mentioned above.

You are not so busy trying to earn your place "doing ministry" that you miss the real ministry to which you are called to.

### #3 – Resurrection morning

The third time this phrase "the disciple whom Jesus loves" comes up is a few days after Christ had died and was buried. It is on resurrection morning.

Mary had just been to the tomb and saw that it was empty and so came back to tell Peter and John.

Let's pick up the narrative from there.

> *"Then she ran and came to Simon Peter, and to the other disciple, whom Jesus loved, and said to them, 'They have taken away the Lord out of the tomb, and we do not know where they have laid Him'" Peter therefore went out, and the other disciple (John), were going to the tomb. So they both ran together, and the other disciple outran Peter and came to the tomb first" (John 20:2-4).*

Both Peter and John heard the news and set out to the tomb to see what happened. The narrative tells us that John outran Peter.

I'm guessing it's because when you have greater intimacy; you have greater desire and motivation.

This greater motivation leads to greater results.
They both ran, but Peter was left in the dust.

Those who know grace always seem to overtake those who follow the law. You see it happen all the time in the church.

Those who are focusing on their love for God get so busy "doing." On the surface it looks good and impressive, but in their heart they feel so far away from God. As a result, it isn't long before they start burning out or start missing out on the real important things in life.

On the other hand, the people who catch and understand grace — and focus on God's love for them — start to really excel in spiritual disciplines and life.

Their prayer life becomes real and fruitful.
Their understanding of the Word comes to life.
Their results in ministry are fruitful.

Not just in Christian matters but in life.
Good things happen to those who know and believe that God loves them.

When you know God's love for you and focus on *that* — rather than your love for God — you are more motivated to do good works, which produce better results.

And how many of us can't use better results in all areas of our life?

## #4 – A Couple of days after the resurrection... a morning on the beach

Christ rose from the dead, but He has been out of the scene for a couple of days. The disciples have just gone fishing. In fact they

had been fishing all night and caught nothing.
(What else is new?)

The sun was rising and they were about to bring in the boats after a full nights work.

> *But when the morning had now come, Jesus stood on the shore; yet the disciples did not know that it was Jesus. Then Jesus said to them, "Children, have you any food?" They answered Him, "No." And He said to them, "Cast the net on the right side of the boat, and you will find some." So they cast, and now they were not able to draw it in because of the multitude of fish. Therefore that disciple whom Jesus loved said to Peter, "It is the Lord!" (John 21:4-7a)*

Who was it that recognized Jesus?
John.

And he was the one who had to tell Peter it was Him.

When you know God's love for you, you have spiritual discernment. You can begin to see and recognize Jesus in all things and all situations—which makes all the difference.

When you focus on the vastness of God's love you realize
how big God really is and that all things really do work out for good for those who love Him.

To most believers, Jesus is just perceived as a solution to their problem. In fact, this has been the dominant way of explaining the story of the Bible in the Western culture for the past several hundred years.

Jesus is the solution.

## Chapter 6: The Real Definition of Love

A solution to their sin problem.
A solution to their sickness problem.
A solution to their depression problem.

It is not that there is anything wrong with this; it's just that He is so much more.

The presentation often begins with sin and the condition of humans being separated from God and without hope in the world. God then came up with a way to fix the mess we find ourselves in. So if we were to draw a continuum of the story of the Bible, Jesus essentially shows up later in the game.

The first Christians didn't see Jesus this way, as if God were somewhere else far away and then cooked up some way to solve the sin problem at the last minute by getting Jesus involved. They believed that Jesus was more than that, that Jesus had actually been present since before creation and had been a part of the story all along.

In the first line of his gospel, John calls Jesus "the Word." The word "Word" here in Greek is the word *logos*, which is where we get the English word "logic."

Logic.
Intelligence.
Design.
The blueprint of creation.

When we speak of these concepts, what we are describing is the way the world is arranged. There is some sort of order beneath the chaos, and some people seem to have a better handle on certain aspects of it than others do. Some understand math, some the human psyche; others can speak clearly and compellingly about the solar system. When we say someone is intelligent, we are saying they have insight as to how things are put together or how they intrinsically work.

The Bible keeps insisting that Jesus is how God put things together. Paul said that Jesus is how God holds all things together [Colossians 1:17]. The Bible points to a Jesus who is—in some mysterious way—behind it all.[24]

Jesus *is* the arrangement. Jesus is the design. Jesus is the intelligence. For a Christian, Jesus' teachings aren't to be followed because they are "a nice way to live a moral life."

They are to be followed because they are the best possible insight into how the world really works. They teach us how things are.

I don't follow Jesus because I think Christianity is the best religion. I follow Jesus because He leads me to ultimate reality. He teaches me to live in tune with how reality is. When Jesus said, "No one can come to the Father except through me" (John 14:6), He was saying that His way, His words, and His life are our connection to how things truly are at the deepest levels of existence.

The point of religion is to help us connect with ultimate reality: God. I love the way Paul puts it in the book of Colossians. He as much as says these religious acts and rituals are shadows of the reality. "The reality... is found in Christ" (Colossians 2:17).

Your entire worldview changes when you recognize Jesus in all things. The world becomes alive to you.

You can see Jesus in the small and big things and how He really does hold the whole world together.

## Chapter 6: The Real Definition of Love

Furthermore, when you can recognize Jesus in all situations, it brings great healing to difficult and trying times of your life.

I know I am not alone when I say this, but I have had a lot of "crap" (that is Greek for unpleasant experiences) happen to me.

Before my twenty-ninth birthday came around I:
- Saw my father experience three heart attacks and two strokes, the last of which took his life
- Saw my mother battle cancer
- Saw my parents lose all they had worked for
- Had several hundred thousand dollars stolen from me through various means by con artists and crooks
- Had my life threatened on multiple accounts by gang bangers and contract killers
- I saw my marriage destroyed by adultery, lies and secrets.
- I lost my house, my life savings and everything I had worked for.

It was gone before my eyes.

And that is the short version.

I don't say this for any other reason except to say that I was able to get through all of that, with a smile on my face, because in everything I saw Jesus.

I was able to let go of the reins in my life and simply focus on His abundant love, realizing that all things truly do work out for good for those who love Him.

The stories of those times in my life are too many to tell, but one particular story comes to mind.

On the day my father died, I had driven him back home from the hospital after his dialysis treatment. My father's kidneys had failed and he was required to be strapped to a dialysis machine for three hours, four times a week, in order to stay alive.

Like always, he went into his room to take a nap upon our return. I was in the room next to his and about thirty minutes into his nap, I heard what sounded like choking come from his room.

I ran over there only to find my dad unresponsive to me calling him. I shook him and called his name but he was unable to respond.

I quickly called 911 and after what seemed like forever, the ambulance arrived.

After running some tests, they put him in the ambulance and said they were taking him to a hospital called Scarborough Grace. I told them that all his medical files were at another hospital called Sunnybrook but they insisted on taking him to Scarborough Grace.

Just before we left, my mother walked in through the front door and I let her know all that was going on.

We jumped in the car and followed the ambulance to the hospital. When we arrived at emergency, he was left in the foyer until paperwork was filled out.

I was scared, confused and frustrated all at the same time.

*Why aren't they doing anything?*
*What is taking so long?*
*Is he going to die?*

## Chapter 6: The Real Definition of Love

After an hour, a doctor finally saw him and then informed us that he had suffered a stroke. He then proceeded to ask us, in case they were not able to revive him, what we wanted to do. We were given the choice of whether to leave him on life support in a vegetative state or "let him pass." These are not questions you ever want anyone asking you about your father.

As my mother and I were contemplating the options, it was as though my father chose for us. A nurse came running into the room to tell us that if we wanted to say goodbye, now would be the time. My father was breathing his last breaths.

We ran into his room and, right after I told him I loved him, the heart-rate monitor flat lined.
Just like that, he was gone.

I collapsed to my knees and started bawling.
The Salvation Army hospital Chaplin came into the room to try to comfort me. I threw him off me, yelling, "WHY, GOD? WHY?"

It wasn't that I didn't know where my father would spend eternity . . . or maybe it was.

How could I be sure?

But more than that, what about all my hours of prayer to see him healed? What about all the "deals" I had with God about keeping him alive? What about all the plans my father had that he would never see come to pass?

He will never meet my wife.
He will never see his grandchildren.
He will never see what I become in my life.

As I am lying prostrate on the hospital floor, sobbing uncontrollably, I felt the hand of God touch my heart.

Within the blink of an eye, I had a vision.
I saw my father . . . with Jesus.

I won't tell you the rest of what I saw. It's too near to my heart. All I can say is, that moment instantly healed me from all pain and regret I had about my father. The ability to see Jesus made all the pain disappear in an instant.

I somehow understood the concept of Jesus in all things, and it completely healed my heart and brought me a deep unexplainable joy.

It was also during that vision that I heard God say some things to me.

First, he showed me that my father passed at Scarborough GRACE hospital. Although I was pushing for the paramedics to take him to Sunnybrook, there was a reason he went to a hospital called Grace. God's grace was revealed that day.

It was my dad's wish that when he passed, it would be instant and painless. I was told that the stroke made him unable to feel any pain; it also, of course, took his life quickly. There wasn't any drawn-out battle in hospital beds or anything like that. He died in his sleep.

Also, the timing was "divine." Had it occurred any earlier that day, we wouldn't have caught my mother coming home from work, in which case she would not have been able to say goodbye.

*Chapter 6: The Real Definition of Love* 77

There are many other details concerning his passing that don't need to be shared. There are even questions that I am still seeking answers to, but what got me through this experience—which was probably one of the most difficult times in my life—was knowing and focusing on the grand love of God.

It gave me spiritual discernment to see Jesus in all things, which brought me great healing and fulfillment.

When you focus on *your* love *for* God, as Peter did, you are often times left with spiritual blindness, unable to see Jesus because the situation in front of you is blocking the way.
Peter couldn't even recognize the Lord.

When you focus on God's love for you, things become clear because your eyes are on Jesus, and everything else fades into the background . . . where it belongs.

### #5 – Resurrection Breakfast

After John recognizes Jesus and He enables them to have another great catch of fish, they bring the fish ashore and Jesus cooks them breakfast. Isn't that nice?

Then Jesus has the famous talk with Peter where he asks Peter if he loves him. He asks this three times and I think Peter finally learns that it was never about *his* love *for* Christ, but *Christ's* love *for him*.

After that discussion, Jesus explains to Peter that he is going to die a martyr's death. He mentioned that Peter would be crucified.

*"This He spoke, signifying by what death he would glorify God.*

*And when He had spoken this, He said to him (Peter), 'Follow Me.' Then Peter, turning around, saw the disciple whom Jesus loved following" (John 21:19-23).*

Even after all that, Peter had to be reminded to follow Jesus. As he looks up, what did he see John already doing?
Following.

John had initiative. That's what Grace gives you.
Peter needed to be told what to do. That is Law.

I come across people all the time who are always praying, asking God what to do next.

Lord, would you lead me in every next little step?

Again on the surface it seems like a really good thing, and I am not saying it isn't. But that is the law. Always having to be told what to do.

Grace imparts love into your heart to where you have initiative to do as your heart leads.

It's time that some of us grow up a little bit and graduate from milk to meat.

It's ok as a child to be continually dependent on your parents' instruction, but sooner or later, you need to grow up and just know what is best and do it with freedom, not because of instruction.

This is what knowing God's love will do for you.

Then Peter, with his big mouth, always has to have the last word.

## Chapter 6: The Real Definition of Love

After Jesus said he will die a martyr's death . . .

> *Peter, seeing him, said to Jesus, "But Lord, what about this man?"*

Peter's like, "Yo man! If I'm gonna die a martyr, what about him (John)?"

> *Jesus said to him, "If I will that he remain till I come, what is that to you? You follow Me." Then this saying went out among the brethren that this disciple would not die.*

Now it's not that John did not die but he was the only disciple to die a natural death. He ended up dying on the Island of Patmos after getting the great Revelation.

Peter was crucified upside down.

Grace is natural.
The law is fulfilled and nailed to the cross.
Are you starting to see the difference between focusing on your love for God rather than His love for you?

Do you see the contrast?

The contrast between law and grace?
And the results that come out of each of the focuses?

Yes, you are supposed to love the Lord with all your heart, soul, mind and strength. But this love cannot come from yourself and your own desires and limited strength.

> *"We love him because he first loved us"* (1 John 4:19).

You must come to the place where you allow, focus on, and

emphasize grace, knowing that God loves you with all His heart and strength.

Practice being loved.

Refer to yourself as "_____ (your name), the son/daughter whom Jesus loves."

I go around telling people that I am God's favorite. And not to be arrogant. Just to practice keeping my focus on the right place... His love for me.

## CHAPTER 7

# ABBA

So far I have been sharing a little part of the journey God took me on while re-teaching me Christianity in the light of Love and Grace.

But the last thing I want to happen is that you get a whole bunch of head knowledge yet not experience the reality of the truths in *your* heart and life.

One of the greatest dangers in Christianity is having a bunch of head knowledge about a particular thing but not living it out in everyday life. This would make us like Pharisees, and Jesus didn't have too many nice things to say about those guys.

What I want to discuss in this chapter is foundational.
It will affect every area of your life.

It is, however, nothing new. It's something we all know about in our head, but what we need to do is transfer this knowledge to a truth.

We need to move it down about twelve inches, into our heart.

My "salvation experience" occurred in 1996 (alone in that room setting up sound equipment). I had attended church my whole life, but it wasn't until that experience at the retreat that things really changed for me. God became more than just something I said I believed in.

You'll remember that it wasn't too long after I got saved that I started ministering in my local youth group.

In 1999, we had our Mission Tour across Canada; my experience during that time started me on this whole "intimacy" thing.

In spite of all this, I *still* felt like something was missing.

I was born again, spirit filled, seeing miracles, ministering Jesus' power to those around me, sharing the message of intimacy, but something was still not right.

This something was missing for several years until Jesus continued to speak and minister to me, taking me deeper into this "revelation of Love."

Several years ago, I was asked to preach to our church's Sunday School Children's Ministry. Something I'll probably never do again. What an experience that was![25]

I was teaching about David and Goliath, and using some of the kids for illustrative purposes. They were David and I was

Goliath. (You can probably tell I didn't yet have kids at this point.) The next thing I knew, I had a bunch of kids attacking me . . . and they wouldn't stop!

I have a whole new respect for Children Ministry leaders and teachers. You need a special gifting for that kind of ministry. One that I do not have.

At the end of the talk, a cute, sweet little girl named Jessica came up to me and asked, "Pastor Nick, what does God look like?"

I began to think about it and realized that this is a question in the hearts of everyone, not just kids. Adults might phrase the question differently, but we all wonder the same thing.

This God, what is He like?

Paul calls God a Father [Rom. 1:7, 8:15, 1 Cor. 1:3].

Did you know that you can be a Christian, yet never really know God as Father.

I spend a lot of time in churches.
I've heard probably over a thousand sermons in my short lifetime and realized that the church is really good at preaching about:
  The power of God
  The expectations of God
  The righteous requirements of God

They are not so good at talking about the love of God.

This is why we have trouble answering that question, "What does God look like?"

If I were to ask you this question, how would you answer?

When I ask kids this question, the answers are usually always similar.

> God is old.
> He has a big white beard.
> He always looks a little angry.

He is like a big cop in the universe watching to see who does wrong so He can throw lightening bolts at them.

The New Covenant, paints a totally different picture of God that very few know and even fewer understand.

## God as a Father

Many people have heard that God is going to send you to hell unless you believe in Jesus. Whether that's true or not, what gets subtly implied is that Jesus "recues" you from this mean and angry God.

That God is angry with the world and Jesus is there to try to calm Him down and appease His anger.

People figure that Jesus loves me (this I know, for the Bible tells me so), but the Father is not quite the same. He is way out there somewhere, too big to understand and really notice us, so I'll just pray to Jesus, love Jesus, hide behind Jesus and have a relationship with Jesus and everything will be okay.

When you listen to the prayers of many people, nuances sneak in there where we are directing prayers towards Jesus, completely

## Chapter 7: Abba

neglecting and forgetting the Father.

Jesus gets painted as the older brother who protects us from the angry Father.

But scripture says that Jesus *points us to* the Father.

The truth is that most people are falling short because they stop at Jesus in their lives.

We feel that if we just "accept Jesus into our heart" (which, again, is not found anywhere in the scriptures) then we'll be fine.

It's as though Jesus is the finish line,
the final answer,
the end all and be all.

Please don't get me wrong; I am not taking anything anyway from Jesus or implying that Christ is not important in our lives.

Christ Himself says:

> *"I am the way, the truth, and the life"* (John 14:6a).

He doesn't stop there though. He goes on to say:

> *"No one comes to the Father except through Me"* (John 14:6b).

Even Jesus was saying, "I am not the end. I am not the finish line." He is saying, "I am the gate. I am the 'starting block.' The 'finish line' is the Father."

In fact, in the four chapters after He says this, Jesus mentions the word "Father" fifty-one times.

His emphasis was on the Father. His very purpose was to introduce the Father to the world, with Jesus being the gateway to this wonderful experience.

Not only does Jesus point us to Father but even Holy Spirit does as well.

Paul, in teaching the Romans about this reality, says,

> *"For you did not receive the spirit of bondage again to fear, but you received the Spirit of adoption by whom we cry out, 'Abba, Father.' The Spirit Himself bears witness with our spirit that we are children of God" (Rom 8:15-16).*

The Spirit is called the Spirit of adoption, with the purpose of making us children of God and allowing us to call Him "Abba" (Daddy).

We have a very special gift in the New Covenant that no on else in the scriptures had.

We have God as a father.[26]

He was never father to anyone else.

Let's look again at what Paul said about this:

> *For as many as are led by the Spirit of God, these are sons (kinship, children) of God. For you did not receive the spirit of bondage again to fear, but you received the Spirit of adoption by whom we cry out, "Abba, Father." The Spirit Himself bears witness with our spirit that we are children of God, and if children, then heirs—heirs of God and joint heirs with Christ (Romans 8: 14-16).*

Paul tells us that we did not receive the spirit of bondage again to fear. This fear Paul is referring to is the fear that people used to have of God under the old covenant. He states that you did not receive that spirit *again* like in the old days, for everyone in the Old Testament had fear of God, and rightly so.

But in the New Covenant you have received the Spirit of adoption that you may cry out *Abba*.

Literally: Daddy.

I find it interesting that God purposely made sure this verse was not translated "Father" but left it the way it was meant to be.

If you go to Israel today, you can hear kids in the playground running around saying "abba, abba."

Not "father" but literally "Daddy."
It is an extremely casual, intimate way to call your father.

The feeling and tone we get from the word father is very formal. In the old movies, little royal British kids would be at tea time addressing their dad as "father."

But for kids who love their dad and know their dad loves them, it's *"Daddy!"*

That's the spirit of adoption, that we would become His children and know His love in such a way that we can have intimacy with Him enough to address Him as Daddy. That is a very different image than most were used to in the Hebrew Scriptures.

God, speaking through the writer to the Corinthian church, even says,

> *"I will be a Father to you, and you will be my sons and daughters, says the Lord Almighty"* (II Corinthians 6:18).

God's desire is children.
Not servants but children.
That is why He has given us this Spirit of adoption.

We have become children of God and can call Him Daddy.
What a revolutionary and amazing thought!

And you know what?
This offends many religious people.

I once took a group to a conference and during the worship and prayer my group was praying to and worshiping "Daddy" and saying it out loud. Then a woman who was close by came to us and said we were being irreverent to God.

"How dare you treat God that way? Blasphemy!" she said.

That is the problem in the churches today.
They are living with the wrong type of relationship with God.
Living under a old covenant.

God wants you to know Him as Daddy. If not, He would have never given us a Spirit of adoption nor left that verse in the Bible.

Remember, this is about relationship . . . about Love.

## As Little Children

While Jesus was walking the earth, He picked up a child and said, *"Assuredly, I say to you, unless you are converted and become as little children, you will by no means enter the kingdom of heaven"* (Matthew 18:3).

That word converted is the Greek work *strepho*. It means to turn/twist right around; reverse and totally change direction.

Jesus is speaking to the Jews who were all there listening and was basically saying, "Look, you have always thought of God as a 'slave master,' someone to be feared and revered, always trying to earn something from Him by aiding by the law. You will never get anything that way. You need to change completely, turn right around and be like a child who knows their daddy loves them, if you want anything to do with God's kingdom (His way of doing things)."

Are you catching what He is saying?

Now, please don't get me wrong.

He *is* a holy God.
(Holy simply means set apart or separated, and has little to do with moral "rightness.")

He is still YHWH. (The unpronounceable name of God, often times referred to as Yahweh.)

And yes He is
*El Shaddai* – the one who is more than enough
*Elohim* – the strong creator
*Jehovah* – the Self Existent One
*Jireh* – our provider
*Raphe* – our healer
*Tsidkenu* – our righteousness

and so many more.

But above it all, all of His names are wrapped up in a name by which we are to know Him—Daddy.

When I have a daughter, she is going to know me as daddy.

I may pastor a church, own several companies, and conduct the various ministries in which I am involved. As such, I may have many titles to many people, but to her it would all be wrapped up in the word "daddy."

Yes, we may know of God as these many different names, characteristics and titles however, to us, it can be all wrapped up in one simple and personal name: daddy.

Think about it.

Do you think my daughter, if she has a nightmare or doesn't feel well in the middle of the night, is going to call out, "*Pastor*!!! Rev Nicholas, I needeth thee in my troubling hour, will thouest please cometh to me!?"

Of course not. It'll be, "*Daddy!*" and with that one word, I will be there in a flash.

She won't need to
  ask perfectly,
  say all the right things,
  prove she really desires me or is hungry for me.

Just one simple call – *Daddy!*
That one word from her mouth is enough to touch and move my heart.

I won't turn away from her, saying, "I'm sorry, you didn't say all the right words. You didn't fast or read the right Scriptures. Therefore I will not give you my attention."

The Spirit came to reveal Daddy to us and give us the Spirit of adoption.

Daddy God.

That has a nice ring to it, doesn't it?
Try it with me . . .
Daddy God.

To some, it might take a while for it to feel comfortable.
To others, it fits just perfectly.
What you have been waiting for this whole time.

Regardless of how you feel about it, make the commitment today to only refer to God as Daddy from here on out.

It'll take some practice, but not only will it help cultivate the proper daddy mentality, it is also the only name by which we are supposed to call Him anyway.

## Manifesting His Name

Jesus, on the night before His death, prayed. Part of His prayer says, "I have manifested Your name to the men whom You have given Me out of the world" (John 17:6).

He is telling the Father that He manifested His name to the disciples. What was the name that Jesus manifested to his disciples? It wasn't any of the Old Testament names. As Jews, they would have already known those.

It had to be a new one. One that they didn't already know.

It was Abba.
God as daddy.

Jesus, in His conversations with His disciples, was perpetually cultivating this spirit of son-ship so that they would begin to know Daddy and what that relationship means for them.

One of the gospel narratives shows us one of those conversations, where Jesus says,

> *Therefore I say to you, do not worry about your life, what you will eat or what you will drink; nor about your body, what you will put on. Is not life more than food and the body more than clothing? Look at the birds of the air, for they neither sow nor reap nor gather into barns; yet your heavenly Father (Daddy) feeds them. Are you not of more value than they? Which of you by worrying can add one cubit to his stature? "So why do you worry about clothing? Consider the lilies of the field, how they grow: they neither toil nor spin; and yet I say to you that even Solomon in all his glory was not arrayed like one of these. Now if God (your Daddy) so clothes the grass of the field, which today is, and tomorrow is thrown into the oven, will He not much more clothe you, O you of little faith? (Matthew 6:25-30)*

He was essentially saying:
  Your Daddy clothes the lilies of the field.
  Your Daddy blessed Solomon in all his splendor.
  Your Daddy killed Goliath.
  Your Daddy parted the sea.

He was teaching His disciples about the heart of the Father in order to cultivate this "daddy" mentality.

## Chapter 7: Abba

In another Gospel narrative, Jesus says, "In that day you will ask in my name. I am not saying that I will ask the Father on your behalf. No, the Father (Daddy) himself loves you because you have loved me and have believed that I came from God" (John 16:26, 27).

Usually the Greek word used when describing God's love is "agape" — His unconditional, unfathomable love.

However, in this particular passage, He used the word *phileo*, which means tender affection, like that of a mother to her child.

This was giving the disciples yet again a totally new understanding of the nature of the Father.

Tender, loving affection, like a parent to a child.

Many people in those days were afraid to pray. (Many people today are afraid to pray too.) They were afraid because of the old spirit of bondage again to fear.
So the disciples often times asked Jesus to pray, but notice how Jesus responds.

He says that that He doesn't need to ask for them, but that they could ask Daddy directly. Why? Because Daddy Himself loves them with tender affection, like a loving parent to a child.

Jesus is again cultivating the "daddy mentality."

God's desire is for us to get to properly know Him as the most perfect, loving and caring father. To have our minds and perceptions changed to see Him for who He really is.

## How Do You See Dad?

The poet in Psalms tells us that the "Lord is gracious and compassionate. Slow to anger and rich in love" (Psalm 145:8).

Dad is gracious.

Do you really believe that?

Not only is He all powerful, holding the universe in His hands, but He is also an all-loving and superabundantly gracious Father whose desire is to bless us with every possible blessing.

The Father loves to give.

Even John 3:16 tells us, "For God so loved the world that He gave." What did He give? His most prized possession
—His one and only Son.

Jesus loves to give.

> *who gave Himself for our sins, (Gal 1:4)*
>
> *who gave Himself a ransom for all (1 Tim 2:6)*
>
> *who gave Himself for us, that He might redeem us (Titus 2:14)*
>
> *I have been crucified with Christ; it is no longer I who live, but Christ lives in me; and the life which I now live in the flesh I live by faith in the Son of God, who loved me and gave Himself for me. (Galatians 2:20)*

Paul tells us in his second letter to the Corinthians that God loves a cheerful giver [2 Corinthians 9:7].

Have you ever wondered why?

Some misread into this, saying it's because He's always "greedy" for our worship, and He always demands from us our very best.

But I say He *loves* a cheerful giver because He Himself *is* a cheerful giver.

Even the word "cheerful" here in Greek is *hilaros*, where we get the English word hilarious. Its root carries the meaning "prompt, gracious, willful, favorable."

That's describes Daddy wonderfully.

Not only does Daddy love us, but He loves to give gifts to us. James tells us that every good and perfect gift comes from the Father [James 1:17].

> *"The thief does not come except to steal, and to kill, and to destroy. I have come that they may have life, and that they may have it more abundantly"* (John 10:10).

It's the thief that comes to steal, kill and destroy.

Don't ever attribute that to God. People often say that God took their child away from them, or God caused the plane to crash, or God caused the sickness in their life.

No! That's the thief.

Scripture says Jesus came to give life and to give it more abundantly. That word "life" in Greek is *zoe* and it means "a full, prosperous life."

He then adds, "and have it more abundantly."

"Abundantly" is *perissos* and it means: "superabundant (in quantity) and superior (in quality); by implication excessive, exceeding abundantly above, more abundantly, advantage, exceedingly, very highly, beyond measure, more, superfluous."

This is what Daddy gives us.

Simply put,
> "He who did not spare His own Son, but delivered Him up for us all, how shall He not with Him also freely give us all things?" (Rom 8:32)

What a great question!

Paul says, God did not spare His own Son but instead gave Him to us. Now if He gave His Son to us, would He not also freely give us all things?

The issue is not whether or not God gives us all things. The issue is, are we willing to *receive* them?

You know, many Christians are terrible receivers.

Do you remember when Jesus and His disciples were about to have dinner (John 13), and He gets up, girds Himself with a towel and begins to wash the feet of His disciples?

When He gets to Peter, Peter of course opens his big mouth and says, "You shall never wash my feet!" (v8). A typical and expected response. He probably felt bad, or thought it wasn't right for the Master to wash the feet of the disciple.

*Chapter 7: Abba* 97

I mean, if Jesus came to you to wash your feet, would you allow Him?

You, like Peter, would probably want to wash His feet instead. But watch how Jesus replies.

He essentially says, "If you don't let me serve you and you can't receive from me, you have no part in me" *(v8b)*.
That's a powerful statement.

God wants us to receive from Him.

***

Or what about the story of Mary and Martha? [Luke 10:38-42]
Jesus comes to their house and Mary ends up sitting at His feet receiving from Him. All the while, Martha is up and about, running all over the place, serving Him.

Finally, Martha gets a little upset with Mary and asks Jesus to say something to her sister; Jesus' response is not what you might think.

He doesn't say, "You're right Martha, Mary should be serving me too." Instead He says, "You (Martha) are worried and troubled about many things. But one thing is needed, and Mary has chosen that good part, which will not be taken away from her" (Luke 10:42).

Now here is a question for consideration.

Which sister do you think made Jesus feel more like God? The one who gave and served or the one who received?

God loves to give.
We just need to learn how to receive.
It is often the most proper response we can give.

As a father, wouldn't your desire be to take care of your family and make them happy in any way you can?

You know, if I could afford it, I would buy my kids anything they ever wanted. Now some people say that would be excessive. That would spoil my children.

A spoiled child has less to do with what you give them and more to do with their character and attitude about what you give them.

But I would love my kids and lavish love on then in every way I could. I would never want a doubt in my children's mind that they could ask for whatever they needed and know that I could provide it. I'm not just talking about materially, but in every way.

If I owned the world, I'd give it to them wrapped in a bow.
Wouldn't you? Isn't that the heart of a perfect, loving, and extravagant father?

Now of course I don't own the world, but our Father does!
He just loves you and His love is extravagant.
If you read the New Testament Scriptures, you know that Daddy has never held anything back from us.

He gave us everything. He gave us Jesus.

> *"What then shall we say to these things? If God (our Daddy) is for us, who can be against us? He who did not spare His own Son, but delivered Him up for us all, how shall He not with Him*

*also freely give us all things?" (Romans 8:31-32)*

Paul tells us that God did not even spare His own Son for us. As a result we can know that He will also freely give us ALL things.

Think about that.

If He gave us Jesus, Heaven's best and greatest gift, how much more will He give us all that we ask or need?

To say that He gave us Jesus, without healing us, or blessing us, or anything else He does for us, is to say that those other things are greater and more valuable than His son Jesus.

If He didn't hold Jesus back, He won't hold anything from Heaven back from His kids.

That concept might not sit well with some people.

People have grown up in different situations which have caused different patterns of thinking, but this is the Father we all need to meet and understand.

## CHAPTER 8

# Distorted Father Images

Some might view God as a distant, impersonal being who is uninterested in our daily lives. The truth is that He is a loving and perfect Father who desires to lavish His extravagant love on us.

I find it amazing that the God and creator of the universe desires intimacy with me.

Even the Old Testament tabernacle is a pictorial representation of how people were to approach God.

Although we don't need to get into all the specific details of it here, we can do a brief overview.

The tabernacle / temple consisted of three areas.
   The Outer Court
   The Inner Court / The Holy Place
   The Holy of Holies (where the Ark of the Covenant was stored and the presence of God resided)

Separating the Holy Place (Inner Court) and the Holy of Holies was a veil.

Only once a year, during a special Jewish festival, could the high priest (after going through a very specific cleaning and preparation process) enter into the Holy of Holies to make an offering to God.

This veil separated God's presence from His people.

Now the narrative of Matthew tells us that when Jesus died on the cross, this veil was torn from top to bottom. When we think of veils, we usually picture something wispy and thin, almost transparent. The temple "veil" was four inches thick!

> "And Jesus cried out again with a loud voice, and yielded up His spirit. Then, behold, the veil of the temple was torn in two from top to bottom . . ." (Mat 27:50-51)

The fact that it was torn from top to bottom indicates that it was God who tore it (not man) and it reveals to us several things.

1) God's presence no longer abided in the Holy of Holies.
The Hebrew ritual was now empty and God was no longer in the tradition.

2) God's desire was to no longer be separated from His people. Through Christ's death, He opened up personal and direct access to God.

Intimacy could now be restored, like in the days of Adam in the garden.

Just imagine if someone (or something) took your kids away from you and you could only interact with them several times a year, and not directly, but through a lawyer and legal procedures.

How would that make you feel?

After Jesus died, God said, "Finally, I am going to rip this veil that for so long separated me from my people." We can begin to see the heart of the Father come out in through this event.

Again, God's desire is for intimacy . . .
a desire to be a Father to His children.
That is why it is so important that we understand God as Dad.

## A Fatherless Generation

The problem however, is that the more I started talking about this truth of God as Daddy, the more I realized that people had a hard time dealing with it.

I couldn't put my finger on it. Why was it difficult for people to understand what seemed like such a life changing and freeing reality? I then realized that the image of "father" in our society doesn't always bring the best thoughts or feelings to mind.

Years ago, one of our congregation members brought a young man named Steve to our service. I was talking a little about the Father heart of God and the whole time he looked a little distraught and upset.

After the service, I approached him to introduce myself. After some small talk, he mentioned to me that he didn't like the idea of God being a father.

He went on to talk about how he had a terrible relationship with his parents and the happiest day of his life was when both his parents died in a car accident.

We live in a fatherless generation.
A generation who doesn't know their fathers.
A generation that is searching for the true love of a father.

I once read somewhere that sixty-nine percent of North American children go to sleep every night in homes where their fathers do not live. Before many of these kids reach the age of 18, most will live their whole childhood apart from their fathers.

Many young people (and older people, for that matter) have poor relationships with their father.

As a result, whether we know it or not, there are inner hurts, pains, patterns of thoughts and expectations imbedded deep in our hearts and minds, distorting our idea of "father."

Fathers were given a great responsibility, giving children an accurate picture of what a father should be. The reason this was so important is that it prepared them to have a healthy and accurate relationship with Father God.

When we have broken and fractured father images, it prevents the complete knowledge and experience of the Father's love.

## What Does "Father" Mean to You?

When you hear or think of the word or concept "father," what do you see and feel? Do you automatically think of protection, provision, warmth and tenderness? Or does that word paint a very different picture for you?

I had a young girl in my ministry and every time we brought up the word father, she would just cry and cry.

See, her father abandoned her family when she was just a young girl. He just left with no notice. Not too long after that, her mother tried to kill herself and left her and her sister basically fending for themselves.

Seeing God as a Father was not only very difficult but brought back feelings of abandonment and bitterness.

How is she supposed to relate to God as a Father?

The truth is, whether we like to admit it or not, we see God through our grid of experiences. Every experience we have, especially in childhood, starts to shape our outlook on life.

When our experiences, especially with our fathers, were not

pleasant ones, improper and distorted impressions of God become deeply imbedded in our subconscious mind.

Good experiences help to lead to proper impressions; bad ones lead to distorted impressions.

## The Little Drummer Boy

When I was probably only four or five years old, our church was putting on a Christmas production. All of the various children's ministry classes were performing some sort of skit or song and this particular year we were doing the "Little Drummer Boy."

I remember specifically that day my mother had dressed me in a bright, multi-colored, one-piece jumpsuit. I thought it was so cool until I came to church and realized everyone was commenting on how funny or "cute" it looked on me.

I was chosen as the little boy to hold the snare drum and hit it on beat to the song, "pa rum pa pum pum," while the rest of the kids walked around me in a circle while singing the song.

I remember looking out into the audience as we were performing and seeing my dad bawling his eyes out, so proud of his little boy.

Well it was either that or he was so embarrassed that his wife dressed me in the funny one-piece, bright, multi-colored jumpsuit. But I like to believe the former.

My father was truly proud of me.

\*\*\*

## Chapter 8: Distorted Father Images

While growing up, I played a lot of sports.
I know many people don't believe me when I say that now, but I have the pictures and trophies to prove it.

My parents were the most supportive.
They never missed a game.

During one hockey game, I got into a fight. Those were my pre-Christian days and I was always fighting. This player "sprayed" our goalie (stopped close to him and sprayed his face with ice) and this is a big no-no in hockey.

I yelled at the guy, and he yelled back and that's when it all started. I had executed all the moves perfectly. It was like it was slow motion. I grabbed his jersey, ripped off his helmet and started wailing on his face.

I think I ended up breaking his nose as there was blood dripping from his nose all over the ice.

I got kicked out of the game (obviously) and as I was being escorted off the ice by the referee, I could hear the other team's parents yelling at me.

I then had to pass by our parent's side and remembering wanting to hide my face in shame as I thought I embarrassed my parents. As I looked up at my dad, he was cheering the loudest, slapping the glass and yelling over to the other parents' side, "That's my boy!"

My dad always put me first. As an only child, I was his prized possession. I really did know what it meant to be loved unconditionally. But being in ministry for some time now, I have come to realize that this is not the norm. I have seen people react violently when I talk about God as Father.

One particular time I was riding the subway in Toronto, and ending up sitting beside a young man who must have been in his late teens or early twenties. We engaged in conversation and somehow got on the topic of God.

He mentioned that he "tried the church thing" but was hurt by people and stopped caring about God and spirituality. I mentioned that Christianity is not just a dry and dead faith where we follow a bunch of code of conducts and that God was like a father, not a taskmaster.

Upon hearing this, he nearly punched me in the face.
He said that if God was anything like his father, he wanted nothing to do with him.

## Categories of Fathers

Ed Piorek, author of *The Father Loves You*,[27] says that our earthly fathers fall into one of four categories.

### The Performance Oriented Father

The performance oriented father gives love according to the performance of the child.

This might sound familiar.

Acceptance, affirmation and affection are attached to the achievement of the child in such areas as chores, education, sports, *et cetera*.

## Chapter 8: Distorted Father Images

Love is given or withdrawn in relation to the child's success in what they do.

It's the idea of, "Do what I say and I'll love you. Disobey or make a mistake and I won't." So this father shows love when things go right, but when things don't live up to his standard, he clearly shows his disapproval.

This type of father doesn't openly forgive or even ask for forgiveness when he makes mistakes.

I knew a guy just like this.

It was one of my old baseball coaches. His son was one of the pitchers on the team and they would come early and leave late from practices so Evan could practice his pitching. And all you could hear was his father, who was catching from behind the plate, yell, "Hit the glove, Son. Hit the Glove."

If Evan threw a strike, it was received with great approval.
"Good job, son! Way to go!" If he happened to throw a miss-pitch outside the strike zone, coach dad would yell "What's wrong with you, boy!? You call yourself a pitcher? You ain't good for anything."

"Hit the glove, Son."
An invitation to "earn" love based on performance.

The result of having this type of father as it translates to our relationship with God is that we think we have to earn God's love. That we have to be a "good Christian" and perform just right in order to receive love.

This is such a prevalent mindset in the church today where people are doing everything they can to earn the love of the Father, not realizing that He loves them regardless. God loves us not because we're lovely, but because He is love.

**The Passive Father**

The passive father doesn't actively demonstrate love to his child. He doesn't speak words of love, nor offer an affectionate physical touch of love. As a result, the developing child is deprived of the emotional nourishment that this demonstrated affection brings.

Fathers in this category are not home much. When they are, they are not emotionally open or available and so they never really demonstrate love.

Sometimes these types of fathers:
   travel lots for work or business,
   are workaholics working long and aren't home very often,
   or are even alcoholics.
Or maybe it's not that at all.

Some fathers were separated by divorce or death and so cannot fulfill the child's needs because they are not there.

Tina and Lin's fathers are examples of this kind of father.

Tina's father passed away when she was just a little girl. Her mother never remarried so she doesn't know what it means to have a father.

Lin's father, on the other hand, was so busy working that he would be out of the country three out of the four weeks in the month until he ended up relocating to another country for work.

The result of the passive father, with regards to our relationship with God, is that we feel God is distant, uninvolved and undemonstrative in His affections.

We know that God is "there," but He is not really interested in our lives and too busy doing whatever it is He does to keep the universe running.

## The Punitive Oriented Father

The punitive father gives some form of abusive pain instead of love. This could be verbal, physical or sexual abuse.

I had a friend named Johnny.
When we were in the sixth grade, I would go over to his house and he would often come to mine.

His dad had a huge toolset and workbench in their garage. It was like he was always building or fixing something.
Johnny loved his dad. Always wanted to be like him.

One day while I was over, we went into the garage to see his dad. Johnny just wanted to help out and be around his dad but he accidentally knocked one of the tools off the table and it hit the ground.

His dad grabbed him and began to yell at him, telling him he was good for nothing, clumsy, and to never come back into the garage again as he didn't want to see him.

This seemed to be a regular occurrence.
Johnny just trying to get close to his father and his father always yelling and threatening him.

The result of this kind of father, with regards to our relationship with God, is that we can see God as abusive, stern, harsh, unforgiving and certainly unloving.

Lastly we have ...

**The Pretty Good Father**

These fathers are generally very loving to their children.
They have good qualities mixed with some less desirable ones but generally are "pretty good."

This is the category my dad fit in.

Growing up, I never questioned whether or not he loved me. It was abundantly clear that my dad loved me. But I did have another set of interesting challenges. My father had me late in life. He was fifty years old. Whenever we went out, people would always think he was my grandfather. This hurt me greatly.

Furthermore, he had come from a war-torn country and arrived here without much education. As a result, while many of the other kids had their father help them with homework and other things growing up, my dad couldn't.

He also fell ill early in my life. I witnessed his first heart attack when I was only four years old. From that point onward, he never had good health.

Growing up, I always knew I was loved, but I had to become independent very quickly. I had to learn to take care of myself; this translated into me knowing that God loved me without question, but I felt that God wasn't able to fully take care of me so I had to do things on my own.

# Chapter 8: Distorted Father Images

The interesting challenge of kids with "pretty good" fathers is overcoming the fact that although our fathers are pretty good, they are not perfect. We often bring that into our relationships with God, thinking of God as good but not perfect.

There are also several other areas in which our fathers can skew our image of God the Father.

For example:
Authority – drunk fathers, or fathers who yell and scream, demanding respect.

Faithfulness – where we have had to live with broken promises from our fathers.

Generosity – we always hear "money doesn't grow on trees" and our fathers withhold from us.

Affection – especially the affectionate touch. Men are usually told to hide their emotions so we think our fathers don't have any.

Communication – I once read somewhere that
58% of communication is through eye contact
35% is tone of voice
7% is words

Only 7%? Think about these ramifications.

## All Kinds of Love

The Greek language has many words for the word "love."

*Agape.* A word used to describe God's love for us. A love that is unconditional and everlasting.

*Phileo*. Tender affection like that of a mother to her child.

*Eros*. Romanic "erotic" love.

*Storge*. This is where we get the understanding of the bird the stork. You know, the one that delivers babies to their parents in a wrap. *Storge* means "family love." Love shared within a family.

If we don't get *storge* from our parents while growing up, it leads to a love deficit in our hearts that looks in other places to be filled. Young people go "looking for love in all the wrong places" in an attempt to fill this *storge* void.

This, of course, makes it difficult for the child to relate to God's perfect love and God as a perfect Father.

Many of us have had the Father misrepresented to us. It is difficult to have a loving relationship with Daddy God if you have wrong views of Him based on poor experiences in your past.

That is why it is difficult for so many to understand and receive God's Father love.

# CHAPTER 9

# Prodigal God

There are two main responses that identify if we have "father issues" and don't truly know the Father's love.

These responses are beautifully outlined for us in a story found in Luke's narrative. It is commonly called the Prodigal Son.[28]

You can find the account in Luke 15:11-32:

*Then He said: "A certain man had two sons." (v.11)*

First, this story is about a certain man.

Many people think this story is about the kid. That's why it's commonly called "The Prodigal Son" but the storyteller here starts by telling us this story is about a man and what he represents—a Father.

The two sons are just examples of people who don't know the love of this father.

> *"And the younger of them said to his father, 'Father, give me the portion of goods that falls to me.' So he divided to them his livelihood." (v.12)*

The younger son asks for the inheritance and the father gives *both of them* (the younger and the older son) his livelihood.

> *"So they both received their portion."*

We need to see this story from a Jewish perspective if we really want to understand what is going on here.

For a son to come to his father and ask for his portion of the inheritance is like saying, "Dad, drop dead" or, "I can't wait for you to die."

In that day—like it is today—you typically only get an inheritance after the father passes away. Even then, only after the lands were sold and accounts were settled. This was an act of total rejection and rebellion.

This is a story about a father who has been totally rejected by his son.

> *"And not many days after, the younger son gathered all together, journeyed to a far country, and there wasted his possessions with prodigal living. But when he had spent all, there arose a severe famine in that land, and he began to be in want. Then he went and joined himself to a citizen of that country, and he sent him into his fields to feed swine." (v.13-15)*

## Chapter 9: Prodigal God

This is the absolute pits for a Jew, to feed pigs for a living and then later eat what the pigs ate. A Jew won't even eat a pig because it is unclean. And now this young man finds himself caring for them and then eating their food to keep from starving.

Notice, too, at this point he had no friends. All his friends left him when all his money ran out.

> *"And he would gladly have filled his stomach with the pods that the swine ate, and no one gave him anything. But when he came to himself, he said, 'How many of my father's hired servants have bread enough and to spare, and I perish with hunger! I will arise and go to my father, and will say to him, "Father, I have sinned against heaven and before you, and I am no longer worthy to be called your son. Make me like one of your hired servants."'"*
> (v. 16-19)

Do you think for a moment that he cared about his father and how he broke his father's heart? Why did he want to become a hired servant? Because he did the math and realized they got more food than he is getting now.

He wasn't thinking about going home for his daddy.
He wanted to go home for his belly.

It was a totally wrong and selfish motivation.

I am pointing this out to bring some clarity to the story.

Many people teach that when the young man came to his mind, he repented and was sorry for all that he did. That is when he came home.

This is not repentance.

He came back because he was hungry.
There was no concern for his father at all in this.

> *"And he arose and came to his father. But when he was still a great way off, his father saw him and had compassion, and ran and fell on his neck (embraced) and kissed him."* (v. 20)

The father RAN!

There are two words in Greek for run.
The first is a jog and the other is a sprint (as in running a race). This father sprinted to his son.

In ancient Jewish culture, anyone older than thirty years old was not supposed to run. It was considered undignified.

\*\*\*

In the 1992 Barcelona Olympics, it was the 400M semi-final heat race. After the race had started, one of the runners, a man named Redman, pulled a hamstring and fell down on the track.

With courage, he struggled to stand up and started limping towards the finish line so he could bravely finish the race. At that moment, a man jumped up out of the stands, leaped over the barrier and ran towards Redman.

Of course the security tried to stop him, but he pushed them out of the way. At this point more security came, but when the runner saw this man, he waved away the security.

This man ran up to him, put his arm around his neck and helped him continue down the track. When the crowd saw what was going on, they turned their attention away from the race leader

## Chapter 9: Prodigal God

and onto this man and Redman.

Thunderous applause arose. Some say it was the loudest cheering in all of the Olympics that year, as this man helped him all the way to the finish line.

Who was this man?
*His father.*

After the father in the Biblical narrative saw his son, he ran and embraced him.

Remember, his son had just come from tending the pigs and probably "stinketh" to high Heaven.
But the father didn't care. He held him close.

After the embrace, he kissed his son.
The Greek word used here meant to kiss repeatedly.

Even though the son ran away, disrespected the father, and came home smelling like pigs, even though it should have been the son who bowed down and kissed the father, it was the father who embraced the son.

That's the love of the Father!

> *"And the son said to him, 'Father, I have sinned against heaven and in your sight, and am no longer worthy to be called your son.'" (v. 21)*

Did the son finish his rehearsed speech? The next line should have been, "Make me like one of your hired servants" but did he say that? Nope! His father didn't let him finish.

Why?

To be a hired servant means you need earn your livelihood. God will never let you earn His love, His goodness, His blessings, His favor, His peace, His joy, His health, His goodness in your life. The father didn't even let him finish his speech.

> *"But the father said to his servants, 'Bring out the <u>BEST</u> robe and put it on him, and put a ring on his hand and sandals on his feet. And bring the fatted calf here and kill it, and let us eat and be merry (party); for this my son was dead and is alive again; he was lost and is found.' And they began to be merry."Now his older son was in the field. And as he came and drew near to the house, he heard music and dancing." (v. 22-25)*

Now I understand how you can hear music, but how do you *hear* dancing? That must have been some kind of celebration.
Love like this throws one serious party.

This story really should be called "The Prodigal Father."

Prodigal means, "recklessly extravagant, giving profusely, lavishly abundant."

That's God!
Maybe different from the God you know, but it's the God of the Bible.

## 2 Sons, 2 Issues

Then the older son comes and asks what's going on.

In brief dialogue, his father explains that his younger brother returned home. The older brother doesn't care.

In fact, he gets mad and tells the father that although he had be faithfully serving him this whole time, he never even got a goat to throw a small party with his friends.

We are never told if this older brother decides to join the party, but it's important to realize here that both sons had issues. Neither son was living in the love of the father.

One runs away from home and wastes money on wild living. The other stays home to perform his religious duty.

The younger son gets caught up with alcohol and sex.
The older keeps busy by working hard and dutifully fulfilling all his obligations.

Both are lost, and neither of them is experiencing intimacy.

The two basic problems people face when they lack the Father's love in their life are that they end up drifting into immorality or they drift into religiosity in their attempts to find love.

One camp tries to find love in all the wrong places.
The other tries to earn love through a lifetime of works.
Both are lost. Both don't know God as "Daddy."

Let's look at the most obvious first . . .

## The Younger Son

A great young man with lots of ambition.
He wanted to make something of himself, be somebody.
 . . . but didn't know his father's love before he went to do it.

He didn't know love and so went "looking for love in all the wrong places."

Many try to fill their need for love with the same things the younger son did, but, like him, they discover that not only do those things fail, but they also distance you from the only one who can help you.

The younger son = immorality—finding fulfillment in the things of the world rather than seeking personal fulfillment in the Father.

It's not that we can't be ambitious in life and seek to do great things. We just need our priorities straight.

> *"But seek first the kingdom of God and His righteousness, and all these things shall be added to you" (Mat 6:33).*

The verse doesn't say, "Seek *only* the kingdom of God."
That's how most people teach it.
Christ says, "Seek *first*." Seek the other things second.

The problem here was not what the younger son was seeking, but the order in which he was seeking it.
That makes all the difference.

Is this you today?

Chasing after all the things that the world has to offer without first knowing the love of the father?

The end of that path is bleak.
Discover His love first.
You will find that nothing else can compare with it.

## Don't Forget the Older Son

Then there is the older son.

This one is a little harder to identify and not really talked about as much in Christian circles.

Why?

Because everything appears to be so good on the outside.
This son did all the right things.

There was a young lady in my church who was your classic "older son."

She led several different ministries.
She was the hardest worker of the bunch.
She was the loudest worshiper.
On the outside, she seemed the most spiritual and the most put "together."

Whenever I see people like this, I need to have a chat with them to see what's really going on. I asked to speak with her, just to tell her to slow down and relax a little. To find out if something else was going on under the surface. And sure enough, she felt like no matter what she did, she never felt good enough.

She, like the older son, was working for love.

He was outside the father's house working *for* him, but not intimate *with* him.

> *"Meanwhile, the older son was in the field. When he came near the house, he heard music and dancing.*

> *"The older brother became angry and refused to go in. So his father went out and pleaded with him. But he answered his father, 'Look! All these years I've been slaving for you and never disobeyed your orders. Yet you never gave me even a young goat so I could celebrate with my friends.'" (v. 25, 27-28)*

Notice he was in the field. He had to come near the house.

He then bursts out saying that for all these years he was slaving away for the father. He felt like everything he was doing was going un-rewarded.

He thought everything was fine because he was DOING what he thought the father wanted. But they were just empty, religious, dead works.

This problem can be called "religiosity."
It can be defined as attempting to earn the love of God, and the blessings of God through works (actions).

Thinking that Christianity is doing and not being.
Religious striving = earning love through good works.

The mentality is that we have to pray more and read the Bible more, do this and that more, be "holier" more in order to please God and be loved by Him.

We think it's enough to be a "good person" or a "good Christian." We go through the rigorous duties and are caught in the cycle of the endless motions of life without ever being intimate with God.

There was a time when I was a youth and I was doing more than my pastor. I felt that if I just did more, God would bless me more (and I wanted more blessing than anyone). If I could only do more, then I would be worthy to receive more.

I had "religion" without relationship and I couldn't find fulfillment. I had tried immorality and that didn't work. So I tried "Christianity" (religiosity) and that didn't work for me either.

The harder I worked for love, the more it eluded me.

Is that you today?

Dad's love is unconditional.

Both sons had access to everything. It was all there for them. But their eyes were on the wrong things.

***

## The Streets of Bangkok

[29]*They say that the first time Sawat went to the top floor of the hotel, he was shocked. He had never dreamed it would be like this. Every room had a window facing into the hallway and in every room sat a girl. Some looked older and they were smiling and laughing, but many of them looked like they couldn't have been more than twelve or thirteen years old. Some even looked younger. They looked nervous, frightened.*

*It was Sawat's first venture into Bangkok's world of prostitution. It all began innocently enough, but soon he was caught up in it, like a small piece of wood in a raging river. It was too powerful for him, too swift and the current too strong.*

*Soon he was selling opium to customers and propositioning tourists in the hotels. He even went so low as to actually help buy and sell young girls, some of them only nine and ten years old.*
*It was a nasty business, and he was one of the most important of the young "businessmen."*

*Sawat became a central figure in one of the world's largest and most loathsome trades: Thailand's sex industry. It is estimated that over 10% of all girls in Thailand end up in prostitution. The top floors of most hotels are used by them, as are the back rooms of many bars.*

*Though the practice is discouraged by the Royal Family, many poorer rural families sell their young daughters to pay off family debts. Who knows what happens to many of these frightened ten-year-olds when they have outlived their "usefulness"?*
*Sawat disgraced his family and dishonored his father's name. He had come to Bangkok to escape the dullness of village life. He found excitement and popularity as he prospered in this sordid lifestyle.*

*But then the bottom dropped out of his world. He hit a string of bad luck: he was robbed and, while trying to climb back to the top, he was arrested. Everything went wrong. The word spread in the underworld that he was a police spy. He finally ended up living in a shanty by the city rubbish dump.*

*Sitting in his little shack, he thought about his family. Especially his father. He remembered the parting words of his father, a simple Christian man from a small village in the south, near the Malaysian border: "I am waiting for you."*
*Would his father still be waiting for him after all he had done to dishonor the family name? Would he receive him home after he*

*had disregarded all he had been taught about God's love? Word had long ago filtered back to his village about his life of crime and sin.*

*Finally, he devised a plan.*
*"Dear Father," he wrote, "I want to come home, but I don't know if you will receive me after all that I have done. I have sinned greatly, Father. Please forgive me. On Saturday night I will be on the train which goes through our village. If you are still waiting for me will you tie a piece of white cloth on the po tree in front of our house?"*

*During the train ride, he thought over his life of evil. He knew his father had every right to refuse to see him. As the train finally neared the village, he was filled with anxiety. What would he do if there was no white piece of cloth on the po tree?*

*Sitting opposite of Sawat was a kind stranger who noticed how nervous his fellow-passenger had become. Finally, Sawat could stand the pressure no longer. The story burst out in a torrent of words. He told the man everything. As they neared the village, Sawat, said, "Oh sir, I cannot bear to look. Can you watch for me? What if my father will not receive me back home?"*

*Sawat buried his face between his knees. "Do you see it sir? It's the house with a po tree."*
*"Young man, your father did not hang one piece of cloth... look! He has covered the whole tree with pieces of white cloth!"*
*He could hardly believe his eyes.*

*There was the tree, almost covered completely with strips of cloth. In the front yard, his old father was dancing up and down, joyously waving a piece of white cloth!*

*His father ran beside the train, and when it stopped at the little station, he threw his arms around his son, embracing him with tears of joy.*

*"I've been waiting for you," he exclaimed!*[i]

# CHAPTER 10

# Daddy Loves You

Daddy loves you today. He really does. Just as He loved you yesterday. Just as He'll love you forever. His love is not based on what you do (or don't do) or how you do it. He just loves you.

And it's with an extravagant love.

The prophet tells us, "Can a mother forget nursing baby and have no compassion on the child of her womb?
Though she may forget, I will not forget you!
See, I have engraved you on the palms of my hands"
(Isaiah 49:15-16).

He is saying that even though some mothers may forget their children, God will never forget us.

He enjoys you.

He takes delight in you.
From the deepest depths of His being, He loves you.

It's like the old saying that goes:
Someone once asked God how much He loved them. God opened up His arms and said "This much" and sent Jesus to spread His open arms while dying on the cross.

Paul says, "But God demonstrates His own love toward us, in that while we were still sinners, Christ died for us" (Romans 5:8).

When did Christ die for us?
While we were still sinners.

When we shook our fists in the face of the very one who gives us breath and life, He loved us so much that He was still willing to pay the price of our sins.

Notice the passage doesn't say "after we earned it" or "after we proved our love," then He loved us and sent His Son to die for us.

No! While we were incapable of loving Him. While we were totally undeserving. It is then that He loved us. And He still does.

Again it's that word *Agape*—unconditional, unmerited love. That is so different from our world's system.

Even our driver's license is based on a merit (point) system. We call them demerit points here in Canada.

When you drive well for a certain number of years, your demerit points go up. If you get a ticket or get into an at-fault accident, your demerit points go down.

How much you pay for your insurance is based on these points. If they go too low, you might even lose your license. All based on performance. This is also reinforced in our typical education system in the form of grades.

It's like everywhere you go, anything good happening to you is based on conditions, based on you performing a certain way to earn it.

This system did not originate with God and it doesn't carry over with Him. He loves and blesses us regardless.

It's not based on our works in any way, but based on His Son's perfect work on the cross.

The poet David says,

> *"As for man, his days are like grass, he flourishes like a flower of the field; the wind blows over it and it is gone, and its place remembers it no more. But from everlasting to everlasting the LORD's love is with those who are His"* (Psalm 103: 15-17).

Isn't that a wonderful word? From everlasting to everlasting. From before the beginning, to time without end, God's love will never run out. It will never run dry.

Human love tends to change, depending on the situation.
I love you today but maybe not tomorrow.
People show love based on many different factors.

But not God.
This love is unconditional.
It is a gift.
Not a reward (for any kind of service).

You cannot earn it,
work for it,
be good enough for it.

There is nothing you can do to have God love you any more or any less than He does right now.

Another prophet, speaking the very voice of God, says, "Yes, I have loved you with an everlasting love; Therefore with lovingkindness I have drawn you" (Jeremiah 31:3).

He loves us with an eternal love.
That would mean (amongst other things) that there was never a time in your life that you were not loved.

Remember that mission tour I was on in 1999? Well there was a young guy with us. Probably the youngest on the team. He was thirteen or so at the time. It was his first time away from home and we were gone for almost four weeks.

When we finally landed back in Toronto, I remember coming down the escalators towards the baggage claim and his entire family was waiting there. Not just his parents, but aunts, uncles, cousins . . . everyone!

They had balloons, and had made signs and were cheering when they saw him. I'm sure he was a little embarrassed but I'm sure he felt the love.

And that is how our Dad is.
The Dad who is in crazy love with his kids.

***

## Chapter 10: Daddy Loves You

In talking about love, the apostle Paul writes:

> *"For I am persuaded that neither death nor life, nor angels nor principalities nor powers, nor things present nor things to come, nor height nor depth, nor any other created thing, shall be able to separate us from the love of God which is in Christ Jesus our Lord"* (Romans 8:38-39).

Nothing can separate us from the love of God?

Nothing?

I used to think if I could just read my Bible more frequently, or pray a little more, or do more ministry . . . then God would love me more. I also thought that if I sinned or fell short in some area of my life, God would love me a little less.

But Paul here says *nothing* can separate from the love of God. Nothing in any realm can have any bearing on God's love for us. Nothing can make Him love us any less.

No devil
No angel
No spirit
No action
No sin
No "nothing"
He loves us no matter what.

Again, because of our experiences, we have a skewed mentality. We often feel that God loves us more when we do well or do all the right things, and that He loves us less when we don't.

This is evidenced by our subtle comments.

If something goes wrong in someone's life, the first question we ask is, "Did you _____ (fill in the blank: sin, not tithe, not be nice to someone, etc)?"

We automatically think that God is punishing us for something we have or haven't done.

The reality is a very different matter altogether.
No matter what you have been through,
no matter what you have done,
no matter how others may see you,
God loves you.

He loves you to "death."
Scriptures tell us, "Greater love has no one than this, than to lay down one's life for his friends" (John 15:13).

The greatest act of love is that you would lay down your life, and Daddy did just that on the cross.

We are told that God is love.

> *"And we have known and believed the love that God has for us. God is love, and he who abides in love abides in God, and God in him" (1 John 4:16).*

It is not that God HAS love; God IS love.
And He gave Himself.

Paul, when describing love, says, "Love is patient, love is kind. It does not envy, it does not boast, it is not proud. It is not rude, it is not self-seeking, it is not easily angered, it keeps no record of wrongs. Love does not delight in evil but rejoices with the truth. It always protects, always trusts, always hopes, always perseveres. Love never fails" (1 Corinthians 13:4-8).

If God is love, then could Paul be describing God here? Can we also read it this way?

God is patient.
God is kind.
God does not envy, He does not boast, He is not proud.
God is not rude.
God is not self-seeking.
God is not easily angered.
He keeps no record of wrongs.
God does not delight in evil, but rejoices with the truth.
He always protects.
He always trusts.
He always hopes.
He always perseveres.

God never fails.

## The Picture in the Store Window

About the time that I got my driver's license, my parents attended monthly meetings about forty-five minutes from our home. I drove them to and from the meetings, which would last from two to three hours. One time I decided that, rather than waiting in the parking lot, I was going to go for a drive. I didn't really know where I was, but figured I could just drive around and try to find something to do.

After driving a little bit, I came across a street that looked vaguely familiar so I took it and ended up at the largest shopping mall in that city, a mall called Square One.

This mall was very elaborate and easy to get lost in. Here is a map so you can see what I'm talking about:

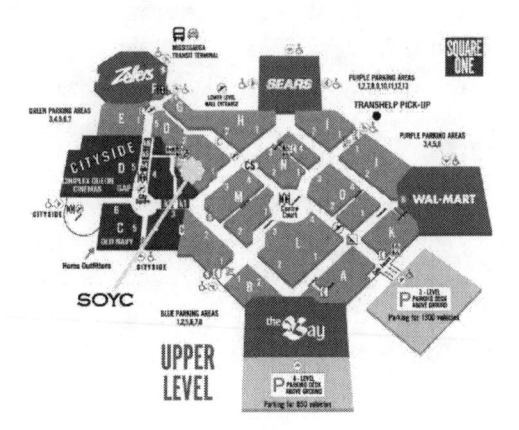

Well, I was a young, "on-fire" Christian and really didn't want to waste my time, so I asked the Lord to use me during this time. I remember sitting on a bench right in front of the food court in a high traffic area.

I prayed, asking Dad to send someone to sit beside me that I could witness to and get saved. (Yes, I was very ambitious.)

After just a little while, a very large man—he must have been three hundred or more pounds—came cussing and swearing and was obviously very upset.

He sat down beside me and, looking all angry, yelled, "What are you looking at?"

I prayed silently,
*Lord I am too young to die here in this mall. I know I said to send someone that I can witness to, but this guy just doesn't seem to want to have any part of anything.*

## Chapter 10: Daddy Loves You

With my voice trembling in fear, I quickly looked away and said, "Nothing sir, sorry."

He got up and left, and I, feeling condemned about my evangelical failure, thought I needed to try a different approach. I often watched Benny Hinn on television at 7am, before school. They would always air his local and international crusades.

I thought, *Benny Hinn is an evangelist. Maybe I should try his techniques.* All I could remember was that every time he yelled, "Touch!" and put forth his hand, people would "fall under the power."

I figured to myself, *This might be worth a try.*

So sitting on my bench, as groups of people would walk by, I would stand, stretch out my hand towards them and yell, "Touch!" expecting that the power of God was going to fall on them and they would fall, start repenting of their sins and get saved right then and there.

Instead I just ended up startling a few people; most just looked at me strangely and continued to walk by.

I wondered what was going wrong.
Why wasn't it working?

I thought back to Benny and realized sometimes he used the word "FIRE!" so figured that's why it wasn't working and I should say "Fire!" instead.

So as the next group walked by, I stood up, stretched out my hand and yelled, "FIRE!" again expecting that the power of God would come fall on these people and they would all fall to the ground in sorrowful "repentance" and I would get them all saved.

But just like that last time, I was only getting a few weird looks while most just ignored me. One person thought I was yelling fire because there was a fire and he started running.

At this point, both of my "evangelism techniques" had failed miserably so I asked the Lord what was happening. Before I could even finish my prayerful thought, I heard the voice of the Lord say to me, *Stand up!*

I stood up.

*Turn left and start walking.*

I turned left and started to walk.

*Turn right*
*Turn left down that hall*
*Turn right over there*
*Walk straight*

After maybe ten minutes of this, I realized that it was about time that my parents' meeting was ending, so I should try to find my car and find my way back.

I told the Lord, "I'm sorry, I don't know what You are up to but I have to go." I had just stepped onto an escalator going down in an attempt to find the exit towards my car. Nearing the bottom, I saw a picture frame store.

Right there, in the middle of the window, was a picture of Jesus holding a little child.

*Chapter 10: Daddy Loves You* 139

As I approached the store, I heard His voice say, *You see that man in that picture? That is Jesus.*

I thought to myself, "No kidding. It doesn't take much to figure that out."

Then the voice continued, *And you see the boy He is holding?*

"Yes," I thought.

*That's you. And I took you on this little "adventure" through the mall just to tell you how much I love you.*

I had tears streaming down my cheeks as my face was pressed against the glass. The people inside the store were looking at me strangely so I quickly wiped my tears and walked away.

This is the kind of Father we have. One who is willing to go out of His way just to show us how much He so dearly loves us.

## It Pleased Him to Bruise Him

Isaiah 53 is the great prophetic passage speaking of Jesus' substitutionary work on the cross.

It's a great read but I want to quickly fast forward to verse 10.

> *Yet it pleased the LORD (YHWH) to bruise Him (Jesus).*

The word "bruise" is the Hebrew word *daka*, which means to crush, destroy, or break to pieces.[30]

Now when I first read this passage, I didn't know what to do with it. It didn't sit so well with me.

I mean, I can begin to understand that God put all of our sins and sicknesses onto Jesus and crushed Him through it (which even in itself is hard to really get your mind around), but I didn't know how it could PLEASE Him to do this to His Son.

It's one thing to *have* to do it. It's another to be *pleased* by it.
It just didn't make sense.

Until I read the first part of Isaiah 53.
The first verse reads, "And to whom has the arm of the LORD (YHWH) been revealed?"

God is saying here that His arm is actually Jesus Christ.

I was suddenly reminded of an experience I had many years ago, which helped me understand this.

After high school, my plan was to move to Texas. I had enrolled in a Bible College there, found a home church to be a part of, and even had my first month's rent paid on an apartment that I would be living at.

Several months before the planned move, I visited to get everything in order. I was staying with some pastor friends of mine. They had a daughter named Jane (not her real name) who I fell in love with and the feeling was mutual with her too.

Now before you make assumptions, Jane was around four years old at the time and the cutest little girl I had ever met. She always had a huge smile and a little raspy voice.

One day, some of the pastors' wives decided to go shopping, so they took me along with them. Jane wanted to be carried everywhere in my arms.

Now this is not a baby we're talking about. She was four years old and she was a little heavy, but she wanted to be carried around rather than pushed in a stroller.

Well, because I thought she was the cutest ever, I did.

Now at that point, I didn't realize how long Texan ladies—especially pastors' wives could actually shop—so it was more than five hours before we were done. That was when we realized that we forgot where the car was parked.

I was tired at this point, but I wanted to be a courteous guest so I took the shopping bags in my hand to carry out to the car.

Jane was really tired as well, and a little cranky (you know how kids can get). When I tried to put her down, she didn't want to go down. So I had all the bags in one hand and Jane in my other. As we began searching for the car, she fell asleep on my shoulder.

By now it was dark outside, no one remembered where the car was parked, we were looking everywhere and we finally realized that it was quite far from where we were.

During this time, my arm had fallen asleep (you know, pins and needles). I was in pain, exhausted and getting a little frustrated.

I could have very easily relieved myself of all this pain by simply waking Jane up and having her walk to the car, but I cared for this kid. When I looked at her, she was so comfortable and peaceful that I just wanted to let her sleep.

Even though my arm was being crushed, because of my love and care of her, it was ok.

The Lord reminded me of this, saying, *Jesus is my arm; and the reason it pleased me to crush Him was because I saw you. And because of my love for you, it pleased me to crush my arm.*

Because of my love for Jane at the time, it pleased me (in a weird little way) to crush my arm that she might be comfortable. That she might be blessed and that she might have rest.

And I began to realize the love of God for you and me.

It pleased God to crush His Son, because of His love for us, His Children. When God turned His back on Jesus, He turned His face towards us.

For the first time, God heard His Son cry, "My God, My God, why have you forsaken me?" (Matthew 27:46).

Nowhere else in the entire scriptures did Jesus refer to God as His "God." It was always His "Father." But here, on the cross, He was taking our place—the place of a sinner.

He called Him "My God" so that you and I could call Him Daddy. That is His love.

*\*\**

In one of Jesus' last prayers on earth to the Father, He prays, " . . . that the world may know that You have sent Me, and have loved them as You have loved Me" (John 17:23).

What amazing words.

"Father, let them know you love them as you love Me."
Notice the word "as" there.
God loves us *as* He loves Jesus.

The same, not less.
WOW!

## A New Take on Isaac

You know, sometimes love is best understood by seeing what we are willing to give up for it.

For example, let's say you have $500 cash in your pocket and you walk into a mall and see an article of clothing that you like. The item costs $400.

So you think about it: *What do I value more, the money or the article of clothing?* The value of the clothes is seen when you are willing to give up your hard-earned money for it.

God loves Jesus.

We are told in many places that Jesus is God's beloved Son, in whom He is well pleased.

You will never really know how much God loves you until you know how much God loves Jesus—because He was willing to give up Jesus for us. God considered you dear and precious enough for Him to give up the one Son He dearly loved.

Do you remember the story of Abraham, when he was asked by God to give up his son Isaac?

It is found in Genesis Chapter 22, verses 1 through 14.[31]
Read it now to get familiar with it.

I remember that when I first heard the story, I thought it was all about Abraham. How loyal and faithful of a guy he was, how he is an example to all of us of someone we should strive to be like.

I would preach messages entitled, "Give Up Your Idols," telling people that if they wanted to follow God, they needed to let go of everything close to them to prove their love for God. I said that God required the thing closest to their heart.

I would quote verses like Matthew 10:37: "Whomever loves their mother or father more than me is not worthy of me" . . . so give up your mamma!

That is not what this passage is saying at all.

That is totally misrepresenting this passage, and this kind of message is promoting a works-based mentality, when really this passage is all about grace.

Let's look at it a little closer here.

> Then He said, "Take now your son, your only son Isaac, whom you love, and go to the land of Moriah, and offer him there as a burnt offering on one of the mountains of which I shall tell you" (Gen 22:2).

First, it seemed a little strange that God would do this. It's almost as though He is rubbing it in.

He starts by saying, "Take now your son."
Now that's bad enough as it is. But God doesn't stop there.

"Your only son."
Yes God, I know which one you are taking about, no need to emphasize it.

And He continues: "the one whom you love."
Okay, I got it! Geeze, do you really need to rub it in like that?

Just a quick side note here.

Isaac was not Abraham's only son. Abraham had another son named Ishmael, yet God only recognized one. Could it be that that which is born of the flesh, God doesn't even recognize, but only that which is born "in the Spirit"?

Anyways, back to the story.

What was going on here?

It was poetry and story telling at its best, in real life.
This was foreshadowing.

When God was saying this to Abraham, He knew that one day God would give up His Son, His only Son, the Son whom He loves in a similar fashion.

Abraham is obedient to all of this. He tells the young servant that is with him, "Stay here with the donkey; the lad and I will go yonder and worship" (Gen 22:5a).

"Go yonder and worship"? Is God from the south?

There is a Bible interpretation method called "the law of first mention." It basically states that the first time a word comes up in the Bible, it has special meaning and helps to define the word for the rest of the Scriptures.

Well, this particular story is the first time both the word "worship" and the word "love" come up, so we are going to learn all about worship and love through this.
And the story is very telling.

The son takes the wood for the offering on his back as he walks up the mountain (sound and look familiar?).

As he gets to the top, he says to his dad, "I see the wood, I see the fire, but where is the sacrifice?"

And I love Abraham's response.

> *"My son, God will provide Himself the lamb for a burnt offering"* (Gen 22:8).

At first glance, we take it at face value. God will provide a lamb for Himself.

However, if you see this with prophetic eyes (as I believe it is meant to be seen), you will understand that He is saying, "God will provide *Himself* - Who will be the lamb for the offering - Jesus Christ."

So they go up and just before Abraham takes his son's life, God stops him and says, "Do not lay your hand on the lad, or do anything to him; for now I know that you love God, since you have not withheld your son, your only son, from Me" (Genesis 22:12).

God said, "I know you love me because you gave up your son for me." He was trying to show us something deeper here. The meaning of love.

And now we can say to God, "Now I know that You love me, because You did not withhold Your son, Your only son, from me."

Remember, "In this is love, not that we loved God, but that He loved us and sent His Son to be the propitiation for our sins" (1 John 4:9-10).

You will never know how much God loves you unless you know how much God loves Jesus, because He gave up Jesus for you.

Scriptures tell us that this happened near the peak of Mount Moriah. This is the place where, many years later, the hill Golgotha stood. The very same place where Jesus was crucified outside the walls of Jerusalem.

I wonder if, when Abraham was walking down from there, he looked back at that spot and saw a vision of Jesus on Calvary.

This story ends up saying, "as it is said to this day, 'In the Mount of the LORD it shall be provided'" (Gen. 22:14).

This sounds a little prophetic again, doesn't it?

Abraham says "shall be" provided. As in the future.
Not that it *was* provided (even though it was) but that it *shall be*.
In the mount of the Lord, it later was provided.
The greatest demonstration of love . . . Jesus Christ.

The greatest act of love towards mankind was demonstrated on the cross.

> *"In this the love of God was manifested toward us, that God has sent His only begotten Son into the world, that we might live through Him. In this is love, not that we loved God, but that He loved us and sent His Son to be the propitiation for our sins" (1 John 4:9-10).*

Paul's prayer when writing to the church in Ephesus was, "that Christ may dwell in your hearts through faith; that you, being rooted and grounded in love, may be able to comprehend with all the saints what is the width and length and depth and height— to know the love of Christ which passes knowledge; that you may be filled with all the fullness of God" (Ephesians 3:17-19).

Paul's prayer was that we would be grounded in the love of Christ. That we would comprehend the multi-dimensional (notice the four dimensions mentioned—width, length, depth and height) love of Christ and know God (intimately) so that we can be filled with the fullness of God.

Notice here too that it says we would know the love *of* Christ, not focusing on our love *for* Christ.

It really is all about love.

## Happy Thought

Do you remember the movie "Hook" with Robin Williams and Dustin Hoffman?

It was a telling of the Peter Pan story.

At one point in the story, the old Peter Pan (played by Robin Williams) is back in Neverland, but he had forgotten how to fly. He was trying all sorts of things and then the Lost Boys said, "If you want to fly, think of your 'Happy Thought'."

And as soon as he thought of his happy thought—his children—he could fly.

Did you know today that you are God's happy thought?

And think about it, what do you think makes God happy?
Serving Him?
Obeying Him?
Doing our Christian "chores"?

At the time of writing this book, I don't have any children yet. But I am praying that God will bless me with at least one daughter who can be daddy's little girl.

Sometimes I imagine what my life will be like with her. What would be my greatest memories?

Would it be when I am in my study and she walks in with a tray, and on it is a newspaper, a glass of water and some food and she says, "Here, father. How else might I serve you today?"

Of course not!

My greatest memories will be when she comes to me and tugs on my pant leg and says "Daddy, up! I wanna play!" and throws her hands up in the sky so I can grab and lift her up.

I would ask, "What do you want to play, honey?"

No matter what her response might be, I would be delighted to join her. (Well, unless she asks me play tea time with her dolls while wearing a pink tutu.)

But I'm pretty sure those would be my greatest memories.

What do you think are God's greatest memories with us?

When we do all these things to serve Him?
Or when we, with a childlike heart, throw our hands up in the air and say, "Daddy, up, I wanna play"?

He really is our wonderful father!

Just as there is a place in our heart that only Dad can fill, there is a place in God's heart that only *you* can fill. Life is just not worth living without the Father's intimate embrace daily.
It's empty. And no one can live—and truly *live*—without it.

We need to be converted and become like little children.

We are His children.

## Chapter 10: Daddy Loves You

To think . . .
    He watches over us.
    He smiles over us.
    He sings to us.
    He knows the hair on our heads.

This is our Dad.

You know, after sharing a talk just like this many years ago, there was a girl who had come to our service.
It was her first time in church.

She met God that day, and that night she wrote the following words.

> *You have touched me,*
> *You have gone into my heart*
> *Into the deepest spaces*
> *The emptiest places*
> *And filled them with love*
> *You have touched me*
> *You have gone into my soul*
> *And fixed my pain*
> *And never again*
> *Will I ever feel that hurt*
> *You have touched me*
> *You have gone into my mind*
> *And erased all that is wrong*
> *And now I belong*
> *And will never be lonely*
> *You have touched me*
> *You have comforted me*
> *and embraced me so dear*
> *And I now hold you so near*

*To my newly fulfilled heart*
*You have touched me*
*You have rejuvenated my spirit*
*And help me to heal*
*and I Know you are real*
*Because you have touched me*[32]

# CHAPTER 11

# Knowing and Believing

His love will change your life.

I remember first time I really experienced God's love.
I was in a church service and it was during worship. I don't remember the song but something started to "break" inside of me.

An overwhelming sense of love swept through my entire body. My heart felt warm and I felt complete love.

I began to tear up and before I knew it, I was bawling.

Not because I was sad, or because I was hurt.
It was joy. Joy like I've never felt before.

I think I ended up crying for two hours before stopping.

My friends who were with me didn't know what was going on. I had great joy, I felt love, and at that time, that was all that mattered to me.

I was once asked to guest speak for a revival meeting in Prince George, British Columbia, a small town where everybody knows each other.

There were about a hundred or so people at this event and in the middle of my sharing, I felt the Lord showing me that there was someone in the room who hadn't smiled in over a year.

I got the feeling that I needed to pray for this person, so I stopped, right in the middle of what I was saying. I asked the group, "Is there someone in here who hasn't smiled in over a year?"

No one immediately put up their hand so I was just going to continue sharing but that feeling came even stronger to my heart.

So I asked again.

This time a young man all the way in the back row lifted up his hand. I ask him if he would come up to the front where I could pray for him.

He agreed.

He walked up slowly, down the middle aisle with a straight look on his face. When he finally made it to the front, I asked him why he hadn't smiled in over a year.

## Chapter 11: Knowing and Believing

He said that there was nothing to smile about. He lost his parents in a boating accident just over a year ago and life just seemed to be in the pits for him ever since.

I then laid my hands on him and the only thing that would come out of my mouth is, "God loves you."
I just kept repeating, "He loves you, He loves you, He loves you."

After about what felt like forever, but it must have been three to five minutes, he just broke down crying. He dropped his face into my shoulder and started to weep. So much so that all the contents of his nose were now on my shoulder.

He fell to his knees and I asked a couple of people to come and continue to pray for him just saying, "God loves you," as I continued to share my message.

About seven minutes later he lets out a loud scream. But a happy one, like he had just won the lottery. He then jumps to his feet, a huge smile on his face, a twinkle in his eye and starts running around the sanctuary laughing and yelling, "God loves me! God loves me!"

Everyone who was there started to cheer.

I cut the message right there. We called the music team up and we broke out into dancing, singing, praising, laughing, yelling . . . it was a party. This lasted for hours until finally we had to shut things down.

I asked him what happened.

He said that he experienced the love of God for the first time in his life and would never be the same again. He went home that night with a huge smile on his face, after over a year of having nothing to be happy about.

I haven't seen or heard from him since so I can't say how he's doing. I'm sure he has had some ups and downs along the way, but one thing is for sure. God's love gave him something to be happy about, and he knew he was loved.

## Know and Believe

*"And we have known and believed the love that God has for us. God is love, and he who abides in love abides in God, and God in him" (1 John 4:16).*

This is such a loaded verse with so many layers of meaning, implications and understanding. But I want to you to notice something specific here that is of paramount importance to this verse.

And we have *known* and *believed*.

Again, by now I am hoping you know that Daddy loves you. But according to this verse, the knowing is just half of it. Not only do we need to *know*, but we need to really *believe* that God loves us.

And these are two very different things. You can know something as a fact or a truth, but you may not believe it.

There are women who are asking their husbands all the time, "Hunny, do you love me? Do you love me? Do you love me?"

Even Eve asked Adam, "Adam, do you love me?"
To which Adam responds, "Who else?" (That was a joke.)

## Chapter 11: Knowing and Believing

It's one thing to *know*. It's another to really *believe*.

The manifestation of the benefit is in the belief of the truth, not necessarily the truth itself. In other words, just knowing a truth does not mean it will be made manifest in your life; it is belief that activates the power of the truth in your life.

The husband loves the wife. That's the truth.
But until she believes it, it's like it doesn't even matter.
It's like that with all of the truths about life.

Step one is knowing the truth.
And it would be of great interest to seek and discover the truths about life, about God, about reality, about the Bible, about all these things.

For example, the truth is that your sins have been forgiven.
Christ came to die for all man's (and woman's) sin, and to forgive all. Also, Christ's work on the cross avails us to every promise and blessing of God [2 Corinthians 1:20].

Step two is truly believing.

> *Jesus said to him, "If you can believe, all things are possible to him who believes (Mark 9:23).*

Notice it doesn't say, "all things are possible to him who knows."

There are many people who know, but don't believe.

We don't have time to discuss "believing," so we'll leave that for another book, but the reality is that we need to both *know* and *believe* God's love for us.

## Beloved

There is a word that I love in the scriptures that I think we need to both know and believe.

*Beloved.*

Throughout all of the New Testament Scriptures, Paul refers to believers as beloved. The word in Greek is *agapetos* and it refers to the object of God's agape love.

Isn't that a beautiful image? We are the object, the very focus that God demonstrates His perfect love towards.
The object of His affection.

That is you who Paul is talking about.
Not just everyone, but *you*!

Read this next phrase out loud . . .
   "I Am God's Beloved."

Didn't that feel good?
He wants us to know that we are so dearly loved.

Even John uses the phrase, "Beloved, I pray that you may prosper in all things and be in health, just as your soul prospers" (3 John 1:2).

Now you may have heard this verse many times before, in various contexts, but the key to being able to prosper in all things is to know and believe that you are God's beloved.

We should not separate that first part of the verse.
When you know and believe this, then of course it makes sense

## Chapter 11: Knowing and Believing

that God's desire is that we prosper and be in health.
It's like any perfect father wanting the best for his children.

He really has given us Heaven's best so we can know and believe that He will also freely give us all the rest.

Great things happen to those who know and believe that God loves them. (Sounds like a good title for a chapter, doesn't it?)

There are all sorts of things happening all around you. The future is, in some ways, a big question mark because of a thousand unforeseen possibilities.

The stock market could crash, there could be a recession, turmoil could erupt in your family, you might be laid off from work . . . but in spite of any possibility or happening, you can still prosper and be in health because you know and believe you are God's beloved. We need to constantly develop and encourage this consciousness of God's love in our lives.

*** 

During that oft-referred-to mission tour, we were on a ferry ride from St. John, Newfoundland, to the mainland, which lasted for several hours. We spent most of the ride on the top deck outside.

After a couple of hours, just about everyone started to get sea sick. People were getting dizzy; others were vomiting over the side of the ferry. It really wasn't a pleasant sight.

Then a local, who was noticing what was happening, told us that the reason we were getting sick was because we were focusing on all the changing waves. If we were to just set our eyes on the horizon, which was constant and unchanging, that would help to stabilize our equilibrium and we wouldn't feel sick anymore.

Sure enough, it worked.

I started to make the connection. When we focus on our unstable love for Christ, which is up some days and down on others, we can lose our footing. If we instead focus on God's love for us, which is unchanging and always constant, we will start to see stability in our lives.

We need to know and believe that we are God's beloved.

## Meanings in Names

Speaking of Beloved, there is a great story in the Hebrew narrative about a little shepherd boy fighting a mighty giant warrior.

You may be familiar with it. It's the story of David and Goliath. It's found in First Samuel Chapter 17 if you want to read the whole thing.[33]

In summary though, you have the Israelites and Philistines (enemies) camped out on two mountains with the Valley Elah in between.
Every day the lead warrior (the champion) of the Philistines, Goliath, would come out and taunt the Israelites, telling them to send their best warrior to come and fight. He had a bunch of unpleasant things to say about them as well.

Now this Goliath character was huge. Some reports say he was over eleven feet tall; most agree that he was at least nine feet tall. So the story goes that David's brothers are there and of course

## Chapter 11: Knowing and Believing

David, the youngest in his eight-brother family, is back at home tending sheep. His dad tells him to go deliver cheese to the boys and that is when David hears these taunts from this giant.

And I love David's response.

> *Then David spoke to the men who stood by him, saying, "What shall be done for the man who kills this Philistine and takes away the reproach from Israel? For who is this uncircumcised Philistine, that he should defy the armies of the living God?"*
> *(1 Samuel 17:26)*

Ever wonder why David said it that way?—Uncircumcised? What did that mean? What was it with this circumcision thing?

The first book in the Bible, a book called Genesis, gives us the answer.

> *"This is My covenant which you shall keep, between Me and you and your descendants after you: Every male child among you shall be circumcised; and you shall be circumcised in the flesh of your foreskins, and it shall be a sign of the covenant between Me and you" (Genesis 17:10-11).*

Circumcision represented covenant.

David knew and believed in the covenant of His people the Jews, and knew that Goliath did not have the same covenant with God, so David gets a little "cheesed" (no pun intended) that this Philistine man would defile the armies of the living God.

You probably already know that names have meanings.

For example, my name, Nicholas, means "victory for the people."

My middle name, Mark, means "strong defender, warlike."

Names in the Bible carried very significant meanings.
It would be in your best interest to find out the meaning of your name, if you do not know it already.

Goliath, big, tall and ugly. No, that's not the meaning of his name. I'm just saying he's big, tall and ugly.
But his name means "stripped, naked."

Maybe that's why David could tell and said, "Who is the uncircumcised Philistine?" ... *Hey, you never know.*

David didn't look at Goliath and see him in all his power and strength and size. David saw him stripped of his might and power. He saw him as a non-covenant enemy of God. Goliath is obviously a "type" of the devil.

The Bible tells us that the devil was stripped (disarmed) from all his power.

> *Having disarmed (stripped) principalities and powers, He made a public spectacle of them, triumphing over them in it (Col 2:14).*

Do you want to know what David means?
> *Beloved.*

It takes a beloved to know his place in God and to knock down and kill the giant.

All of Israel trembled at the sight of this big Goliath. They didn't know they were loved. They didn't know they were in covenant.

Or maybe they knew but they didn't believe.

## Chapter 11: Knowing and Believing

David, on the other hand—who knew and believed he was loved—destroyed his enemy.

Great things happen to those who know and believe they are loved by God.

After killing the giant, by immobilizing him with a stone and then cutting off his head, David takes Goliath's head to Jerusalem [1 Samuel 15:54a].

Why would he do that?

Some scholars and Rabbis agree that David buried Goliath's head in the hills outside the walls of Jerusalem.

They say that the hills were eventually called *Gol Goliath*.
Later revised to Golgotha—"the place of the skull"
— Goliath's skull.

Because Jesus, the greater David, would one day come and be crucified at the place of the skull.

> *So the soldiers took charge of Jesus. Carrying his own cross, he went out to the place of the Skull (which in Aramaic is called Golgotha) (Luke 19:17).*

The picture here is of the greater son of David crushing a greater enemy, not Goliath, but the devil, for all of us.

This fulfills the early prophecy of in Genesis: "And I will put enmity between you and the woman, And between your seed and her Seed; He shall bruise your head, And you shall bruise His heel" (Genesis 3:15.)

This was just one thing that David accomplished knowing and believing he was beloved.

His life is truly an amazing story. I encourage you to read about him to see what can be done when you know and believe the love of God in your life.

There are also two times in the Scriptures where God refers to Jesus as the beloved. Let's take a look at them.

## Baptism and Beyond

The first time is at the rivers of Jordon at the waters of His baptism.

> *When He had been baptized, Jesus came up immediately from the water; and behold, the heavens were opened to Him, and He saw the Spirit of God descending like a dove and alighting upon Him. And suddenly a voice came from heaven, saying, "This is My beloved Son, in whom I am well pleased" (Mat 3:16-17).*

Jesus was God's beloved.

Next verse:
> *Then Jesus was led up by the Spirit into the wilderness to be tempted by the devil . . . Now when the tempter came to Him, he said, "If You are the Son of God, command that these stones become bread" (Mat 4:1, 3).*

So Jesus goes to the wilderness and is tempted by the devil. A few verses later, another temptation.

> *. . . and said to Him, "If You are the Son of God, throw Yourself*

## Chapter 11: Knowing and Believing

> *down. For it is written: 'He shall give His angels charge over you,' and,' In their hands they shall bear you up, Lest you dash your foot against a stone'" (Mat 4:6).*

If you read these temptations closely, you'll notice that the devil dropped one word.

Jesus was at the waters of baptism and had just heard from the Father, "You are my *beloved* Son." But when the devil came against Jesus here, he dropped the word "beloved."

Why?

Could it be that the temptation would be counter productive if he reminds Jesus that He is His beloved?

I think so.

If he confirmed that Christ is God's beloved before he tried to tempt Him, it would be to no avail. (Although it was still to no avail, thank God.)

And the same goes for us. The devil doesn't want you to know that you are loved by God.
He'll make you feel that you are not really loved by God.

How could He love you? After all, look at all you do and don't do. You don't deserve His love.

He knows that if you start to doubt God's love, you begin to question everything about your life and you would be standing on unstable ground.

However, those who know they are beloved cannot be shaken.

Imagine the effect on your mind and heart if you were to really know and believe that God loves you.

No one and nothing would be able to shake you. No matter what happens, you can just say, "Yes, but I am God's beloved."

Let's look at the next place where God the Father spoke about Jesus and said "This is my beloved."

It is at the Mount of Transfiguration.

> *"Now after six days Jesus took Peter, James, and John his brother, led them up on a high mountain by themselves; 2 and He was transfigured before them. His face shone like the sun, and His clothes became as white as the light" (Matthew 17:1-2).*

Now on a side note, why was it that Jesus took Peter, James and John?

Every detail in the scriptures is important and names have meanings. You should really study names as you come across them in the scriptures.

We already saw the significance of the meaning of names with David and Goliath. A picture of Jesus (the beloved) verses the devil (stripped one).

Here is another example.

Lazarus is the Greek name "Eleazar" in Hebrew
Lazarus/Eleazar means "helper."
Or more specifically, *the Lord's* helper.

In the story where Jesus raised Lazarus from the dead, Jesus says,

"Take away the stone" . . . Now when He said these things, He cried with a loud voice, "Lazarus, come forth!" (John 11:39, 43).

Now there are some deep meanings and implications here if we pay attention to names.

Again, Lazarus means Lord's helper. Who is called "the Helper" (*paraclete*) in the scriptures by Jesus?
    The Holy Spirit.

Jesus cries out, "Lazarus, come forth!" In order for the "helper" to come forth, what had to happen? The stone has to be rolled away.

This could imply two things.

First, that Jesus had to be resurrected: the stone would have to be rolled away for the Holy Spirit to come, which would fulfill His promise.

But also, what does the stone represent?
The Law.

The law had to be taken away in order for the Holy Spirit to come, which Jesus did during His death on the cross.

Colossians describes what happened:

> "... *having wiped out the handwriting of requirements that was against us (the law), which was contrary to us. And He has taken it out of the way, having nailed it to the cross*" (Colossians 2:14).

The law—the stone—was taken out of the way
Just like the previous cry, "Take away the stone."
Then He called the Helper forth—the Holy Spirit.

***

Since we're talking about names, let me just give you one more interesting finding.

This one is courtesy of Chuck Missler.[34]

In Genesis Chapter five we have the genealogy of Adam through Noah. I am not going to re-write it here (it's long and frankly quite boring), at least at first glance.

For the sake of time, I will just list the names in the genealogy in the order that they appear.

Adam
Seth
Enosh
Kenan
Mahalalel
Jared
Enoch
Methuselah
Lamech
Noah

Again, at first glance, it doesn't seem very impressive, right? Just a boring genealogy.

But remember, every time you come across a name it'd be good to look up the meaning.

So let's see the names, but this time with the English meanings beside them.

## Chapter 11: Knowing and Believing

| Hebrew | English |
|---|---|
| **Adam** | Man |
| **Seth** | Appointed |
| **Enosh** | Mortal |
| **Kenan** | Sparrow |
| **Mahalalel** | The Blessed God |
| **Jared** | Shall come down |
| **Enoch** | Teaching |
| **Methuselah** | HIs death shall bring |
| **Lamech** | The Despairing |
| **Noah** | Rest, or comfort |

If we were to read just the English names in a sentence that would make sense, it would read:

Man (is) appointed mortal sorrow; (but) the Blessed God shall come down teaching (that) His death shall bring (the) despairing rest.

The Gospel message tucked away right there in Genesis 5.

Isn't that great?

Anyways, back to what we were saying.

So why did Jesus take Peter, James and John up to the mount of transfiguration?

Peter in Greek means "stone."
James means "supplanter" (to replace, to take the place of, remove, succeed).
John means "grace."

In the order that Jesus took them, it means that the law (Peter the stone) has been replaced (James) by grace (John).

The law was replaced by grace on the mountain where Jesus was. Ironically enough, this is the same mountain where Moses, many years earlier, received the Law and gave it to the people.

Thousands of years later, Jesus brought grace at that same mountain.

> *For the law was given through Moses, but grace and truth came through Jesus Christ (John 1:17).*

Isn't that awesome?

## More Good Things

Good things happen to those who know and believe that God loves them.

Let's just look at a few more benefits of understanding this simple truth.

### Prayer

The disciples were wanting to learn how to pray properly.

> *Now it came to pass, as He was praying in a certain place, when He ceased, that one of His disciples said to Him, "Lord, teach us to pray" (Matthew 6:5).*

Jesus responds: "in this manner, therefore, pray:"
He then goes into what we now call the Lord's prayer.
It starts by saying, "Our Father . . ."

Notice that the entire prayer in contingent upon knowing and understanding the revelation of the first two words of the whole prayer: Our Father.

Jesus, in teaching His Jewish disciples how to pray, starts by saying, "If you want to know anything about prayer, you have to know God as Father."

The fruitfulness and vitality of our prayer life is dependent upon our knowing God as Father and realizing His love for us.

## Faith
What about Faith?

> *"For in Christ Jesus neither circumcision nor uncircumcision avails anything, but faith working through love" (Galatians 5:6).*

Paul tells us here that faith works through love.
What that essentially means is that when you know you're loved, faith flows.

Doesn't that make sense?

It's hard to have faith in someone you fear or don't know.
But you can have unlimited faith when you know that the God of the universe is your Daddy and when you believe that He loves you with an extravagant love, a love that promises to freely give us all things.

I walk around knowing that God is my Daddy and He loves me and always wants the best for me. As a result, I can have faith in God's best for me and others.

Just the other day I was guest speaking at a friend's Church

Service. After the service a young girl came up to me and said she had been in a car accident just that week and ever since, her neck had been troubling her.

She asked if I could pray for her healing.

Now if I didn't know that I was God's beloved, I would have balked at this opportunity. I would not have been able to say with great faith that my prayers would avail anything. But since I knew I was so dearly loved, faith was already in my heart. I laid my hands on her neck, and in just a few seconds she was completely healed.

Knowing you are beloved springs up faith.

## Healing
And what of Healing?

Now healing is a greatly misunderstood and sensitive issue in the body of Christ so we won't spend too much time here talking about. (We'll save it for another book.)

But we do know the most quoted verse that pertains to healing. I heard this verse repeated so many times growing up in church.
  " . . . *by his stripes you were healed*" (1 Pet 2:24).

I hear people repeating this over and over again (they call it confessing it), thinking that by saying it over and over again, it will some how magically do something in their life and bring healing.

The power of this verse is not just in the confession of it but in knowing the truth behind it.

## Chapter 11: Knowing and Believing

Yes, Jesus was whipped brutally on the flogging post (as we discussed before), and yes, that was for our healing; the question is, why did He endure all that?

Because He loves us.
For He so loved us that He would put Himself through that kind of agony.

That's where our faith through love comes in.
Knowing that He loves us so much that He would go through that gives us the faith we need to receive our healing. Love is the source of everything.

Even Paul says, *"And my God shall supply all your need according to His riches in glory by Christ Jesus"*
*(Philippians 4:19).*

Why? Because He loves us!

Every blessing from God is because of His love.

> *" . . . but the LORD your God turned the curse into a blessing for you, because the LORD your God loves you"* *(Deuteronomy 23:5).*

The blessings aren't because we have earned it or deserved it but because of His love.

> *"Yet in all these things we are more than conquerors through Him who loved us" (Romans 8:37).*

We are more than conquerors!

First, what does that even mean?

Do you remember years ago when Mike Tyson fought Evander Holyfield for the world heavyweight title in boxing? The day Mike Tyson bit off a piece of Evander's ear?

Well, that day, Evander came home the victor, the conqueror. He fought and he won. Not only did he bring home the belt, but he brought home millions in prize money. Again, a conqueror.

But do you know who was *more than* a conqueror?
His wife.

Without even having to fight, she got to spend some of those winnings.

Paul tells us that without having to fight, or pay the penalty for our own shortcomings, we get to share in the victory of Christ.
Jesus was a conqueror.

We are more than conquerors.

How?

The verse says, "through Him who loved us."
It's all about knowing and believing His love.
Ephesians Chapter 3, verse 20, says, "Now to Him who is able to do exceedingly abundantly above all that we ask or think, according to the power that works in us."

Exceedingly
Abundantly
Above
All that we can ask or think?

Wow, what a promise!

But how?

The verses directly before this one talk about being rooted and grounded in the four-dimensional love of God. The promise is appropriated only for those who know God's love for them.

***

When you are conscious of God's love for you, you don't even need to pray or have faith because good things start to happen all around you based on nothing more than your mindset and the laws of the universe.

He'll go beyond what you can ask or think.
Great things happen to those who know and believe they are loved by God.

Can I tell you something?

Do you know why some people are depressed?
Why some are stressed?
Why some are sick?
Why some experience difficulty in areas of their life?

Sometimes it is because they are believing a lie somewhere in their life, so they don't really know and believe how much God loves them and that He freely gives them all things.
Believe it today.

> "... to the praise of the glory of His grace, by which He made us accepted in the Beloved" (Ephesians 1:6).

The word "accepted" here is *charistoo* and it means "highly favored in the Beloved."

We are highly favored (blessed) in the Beloved.

CHAPTER 12

# What now?

If you have spent any time in church, you have probably heard that faith without works is "dead."

It's taken from the book of James, and what James goes on to say is that if you have faith but you do not have actions that correspond with your faith, then your faith is "dead."

That makes sense, doesn't it?

If you call yourself a swimmer, but never get into the water, you aren't really a swimmer. You can have the Speedo (not always a pretty sight), the goggles and the shower cap looking thing, but if you are not ever in the water, you are not a swimmer.

We have looked at the essence of love.
First, that Dad desires intimacy with us.

Next, that we need to focus first on His super abundant love for us. Then, because of His love for us, we can love in return.

But what then?

The Scriptures say that the greatest command is to love God with our all (heart, soul, mind and strength).

But it follows that up by saying the second command is just like it: that we should love our neighbor as our self.

## Who is our Neighbor?

This is the same question a young lawyer asked Jesus when hearing this command[35] Jesus responds by telling a story that we know as "the Good Samaritan."

A man on his travels gets mugged, beaten, stripped of his clothing and left half dead. Two religious people walk right on by, ignoring the man and passing by on the other side.

Then a Samaritan comes by. Samaritans and Jews generally despised each other, but this Samaritan man helped the injured Jewish man.

There is a lot to read into this story, but the bottom line is that we are called to love our neighbor.

Who is our neighbor?
The world around us.
And those at our side.

*Chapter 12: What Now?* 179

## Love Changing Lives

I heard about a man named Scott Harrison.

He worked as an events promoter in New York City for years. He knew everybody. His job was to get the important people, the wealthy people, the influential people, and the pretty people, all in the same room, or at the same club, or at the same party . . . at the same time.

His job essentially was to know everybody and anybody who is anybody on the "scene." Scott was sponsored by certain beverage companies and paid thousands of dollars a month just to be seen in public drinking a particular brand of beverage.

He talked about how he got so good at projecting a particular type of image that, when his picture was being taken, he would tilt his wrist in just the right degree so that the photograph would reveal that, yes, he was in fact wearing a Rolex.

He spent 10 years (after graduating from NYC) throwing lavish parties for the likes of MTV, VH1, Bacardi and Elle. He described this as a time when he was "chasing after models," mingling with the New York City elite and indulging in illicit drugs, including cocaine and ecstasy.

When he was 28, he had a "crisis of conscience" during a vacation in Uruguay. He had an epiphany about his job and life: "I was selling selfishness and decadence." He recalled feeling like "the most selfish, sycophantic and miserable human being" and "the worst person I knew."

In August 2004, Scott quit his job and volunteered as a photojournalist for a Christian ministry called Mercy Ships, which operates a fleet of hospital ships offering free healthcare throughout the world. He served aboard the Mercy Ship Anastasis in West Africa, taking over 60,000 photos in 13 months.

He then had an encounter with the love of God; that very same love then began to spill over into the world that was around him. During his two years with Mercy Ships, he was exposed to the harsh conditions of the impoverished in Liberia. He realized that 80% of all the diseases they encountered were attributable to unsafe water and poor sanitation. He wanted to commit to a life of service, and decided that the lack of clean water was the biggest obstacle facing the poor in developing countries.

Scott founded **charity:water** on September 7, 2006, on the night of his 31st birthday. In lieu of receiving gifts, he charged his friends $20 each to attend his party at a yet unopened nightclub. He raised $15,000 that night, which went towards fixing three wells and building three more at a refugee camp in Northern Uganda.

charity:water uses all public donations to directly fund water projects such as building wells and sanitation facilities. Since its founding, charity: water has established 25 local partnerships, funded approximately 3,962 projects in 19 countries and provided roughly 1.8 million people with clean water. The organization's goal is to bring clean water to 100 million people by 2020.[36]

He goes on to say:

> There's a biblical parable about a man beaten near death by robbers. He's stripped naked and lying roadside. Most people pass him by, but one man stops. He picks him up and bandages his wounds. He puts him on his horse and walks alongside until they reach an inn. He checks him in and throws down his Amex. 'Whatever he needs until he gets better.'
> Because he could.

> *The dictionary defines charity as the act of giving voluntarily to those in need. It's taken from the word caritas, or simply, love. In Colossians Chapter 3, the Bible instructs readers to "put on charity, which is the bond of perfectness."*
> *Although I'm still not sure what that means, I love the idea. To wear charity.* [37]

## Abide in My Love

> *"As the Father loved Me, I also have loved you; abide in My love" (John 15:9).*

As we bring to a close our discussion on the love of God and living in that love, I would like to point out that Jesus tells us here that we are to constantly abide (continue, remain) in His love.

We are never to wander outside the love of God.

The love of God is our safe place. It's where we find truth. It's where we find grace.

The question is, how do we remain, abide, continue . . . in His love? Fortunately, Jesus answers that question in the very next line.

> *"If you keep My commandments, you will abide in My love, just as I have kept My Father's commandments and abide in His love" (John 15:10).*

Jesus tells us that in order to remain in God's love, we need to keep and obey His commandments.

Wait a second!

Didn't we come to the conclusion that the commandments were not something we could keep? How could Jesus tell us to keep His commandments if we want to remain in His love? Sounds like an impossible task.

Unless we keep reading . . .

What is the commandment that Christ calls us to keep?

All of them?
Some of them?
Just the Ten Commandments?
The ones found in Deuteronomy? (I certainly hope not!)
What about the ones about not eating pig? (I hope not that one as well!)

What is the command that He is taking about in this context? Fortunately, Jesus then tells us what commandment He is talking about in the following verse.

> *"This is My commandment, that you love one another as I have loved you" (John 15:12).*

There is a sequence here we need to pay attention to.

First, we are to remain in His love.
Second, we do that by keeping His commandments.
Third, the commandment He is referring to is to love one another.

Isn't that amazing? By loving one another, we are remaining in the love of God.

But then that begs the question (I am starting to feel like the young lawyer that is always questioning the meaning of what

Jesus is saying),"What does it mean to love one another? What is the measure that we use to gauge this?"

The answer is yet again found in the next verse.

> *"Greater love has no one than this, than to lay down one's life for his friends"* (John 15:13).

What?!

For me to remain in God's love I need to offer my life in martyrdom for my friends?

I guess that makes sense, right? If I die, I get to be with Jesus in eternity, which would be in His love.
Ok then, off with my head!

Are you with me? Will you lay down your life too?
But is that what Christ really means?

The word for "lay down" in the Greek is *tithemi,* which means (amongst other things) "to set forth and serve."
To live for.

Laying down our life then, means to serve and set forth our lives to be a blessing to others. To give of our strength, our time, our efforts to help and serve others.

Once this love has been truly experienced, the natural response is to share that with the world.

> *"A new commandment I give to you, that you love one another; as I have loved you, that you also love one another"* (John 13:34).

Love one another?

There was a young couple that was hit hard by the recent economic downturn that many of us in the North American world experienced. The wife lost her job and the husband's hours were cut. Things got so bad that it was difficult to even put food on the table for the kids.

Another couple in their church heard about this and felt it was unacceptable that this couple was struggling to put food on the table. They called the struggling couple and arranged to meet them the following morning at 9:00am at one of those large, big-box, wholesale stores.

The next morning they met them and said, "We are going to feed you and take care of your groceries and household needs until you are able to get back on your feet."

They ended up spending nine hundred dollars that day stocking this family up with everything they would need for at least a few months.

As the story was conveyed to me, they said that their minivan limped out of the parking lot being so heavy weighed down with food.

*** 

There was a woman who was walking down the sidewalk with a shopping cart full of what looked like household goods, and two kids. She didn't look like she was in good shape with the hot summer sun beating down on her.

A woman (who is very familiar with the loving grace of God) was

## Chapter 12: What Now?

working in her front garden as she saw this woman with her kids and the shopping cart passing by.

She just knew that she couldn't let this woman pass by without entering into her story.
"What are you doing?" she asked.
"Moving," the woman replied.
"Moving? Like this? No you're not," and handed her car keys to this lady."Just bring it back when you're done."

A few hours later, the woman returned, and handed back the keys to the car with the statement, "No one has ever trusted me like this before."[38]

\*\*\*

There was a group of young people who went to Rwanda a few years ago for a short-term mission trip. They went hiking in the slums of Kigali with a woman named Pauline. Pauline spend her free time caring for people who are about to die of HIV/AIDS.

She agreed to take them to visit one of her friends who had only hours to live. They hiked through the slum for what seemed like miles, and as they got farther in, the roads became smaller and smaller until all they had to walk on were narrow trails with sewage crisscrossing in streams that ran beside, and sometimes under the tiny shacks.

Eventually they ended up in a dirt-floored, one-room shack about six-by-six feet. A woman was lying under so many blankets that all they could see was her mouth and eyes. Her name was Jacqueline. Pauline had become her friend and had been visiting her consistently for the past few months. As the group knelt down on the floor, they watched Pauline, standing in the corner, weeping. Her friend was going to die soon.

In this dark place, Pauline's love and compassion were simply . . . bigger. More.

It was as if the smallest amount of light was infinitely more powerful than the massive amount of dark.

Jacqueline felt so deeply loved as she was embraced by Pauline in her last few minutes of life.[39]

*** 

A Christian is at their best when they give themselves away. This is because blessing is always instrumental.

Let me explain.
In Genesis 12, God tells a man named Abram that He's going to bless him, and through him, He is going to bless the whole world.

God wants to use Abram (whose name was later changed to Abraham), to flow through him, to have him be the conduit through whom God can love and bless everybody else. Abraham here is just a vessel.

God doesn't choose people just so they'll feel good about themselves or secure in their standing with God or anybody else. God chooses people whom He can use to bless other people. The point is never about the person. The point is that person serving others, making their lives better, revealing the love of God.

You'll also notice that this calling on Abraham was universal. It is for everybody. All kinds of people all over the place were eventually going to be blessed by God through Abraham. There were no boundaries to this wonderful blessing.

Jesus continues this idea in many of His teachings.

In the book of Luke He says, "I am among you as one who serves." He not only refers to Himself as a servant, sent to serve others, but He also teaches His disciples that the greatest in His kingdom are the ones who serve.

For Jesus, everything is upside down. Or perhaps really right side up. The best and greatest and most important are the ones who humble themselves, set their needs and desires aside, and selflessly serve others.

So what is a person living this way called?
A Christian.

What is a group of people living this way called?
The Church.

This is the true church.

The church doesn't exist for itself and neither does the Christian. They exist to serve the world. It's not ultimately about the church; it's about the people God wants to bless *through* the church. When the Christian, and the church, loses sight of this, it loses its heart.

This is especially true today in the world we live in where so many people are hostile to Christians and for good reason. We need to reclaim the church as a medium for blessing the world, not only because that is what Jesus intended from the beginning, but also because serving people is the only way the world will see God the way He should be seen.

That is why it is so toxic for the gospel when Christians picket and boycott and complain about how bad the world is. This doesn't help anything or anyone. It makes it worse. It isn't the kind of voice Jesus wants us to have in the world. It's actually damaging.

Why blame the dark for being dark? It is far more helpful to ask why the light isn't as bright as it could be.

A very powerful thing happens when the church surrenders its desire to convert people and instead convinces them to join a living, breathing body that is doing its best to change the world. It is when the church gives itself away in radical acts of love and service, expecting nothing in return, that the way of Jesus is most vividly put on display.

To do this, the church must stop thinking about everybody primarily in the categories of in or out, saved or not, believer or non-believer. Besides the fact that these terms are offensive to those who are the "un" and the "non," they work against Jesus' teaching about how we are to treat each other.

Love your neighbor as yourself.

And our neighbor can be anybody. We need to stop serving people with a hidden agenda. It's like we do good only to be able to convert people to the faith.

That means there is an agenda. And when there is an agenda, it isn't really love, is it? It's something else.

We have to rediscover love. Period.
Love that loves because it is what Jesus teaches us to do. Not only that, but because it is the love that He shows us.

## Inner City Love

I recently read of a woman named Jennifer who decided to move into the roughest neighborhood in her city to try to help people get out of the cycle of poverty and despair. She spoke of the kids she was tutoring and the families they came from and how great the needs were.

Some other women in her church heard about Jennifer and asked her for lists of what exactly the families in her neighborhood need. (One of the families wrote on their list "heat".) The women then circulated the lists until they found people who could meet every one of the needs. It's like an underground mom mafia network.

Jennifer said at last count they had helped 430 families, and they are making plans to expand their network.

Jesus loves you, and here is a toaster.

## Tsunami T-Shirts

When Japan was hit with a Tsunami that shook their entire country a young girl in my church named Michelle decided to put her design talents to work and designed this t-shirt to fundraise for the aid efforts in Japan.
She took the time and effort not only to create it, but also to go to Christian concerts and various other events to sell them.

Her efforts translated into thousands of dollars that were sent to help people she didn't even know.

## 1000 Cupcakes

Another young lady from my church, Rivonny, used her passion and talent for baking to start a campaign she called 1000 Cupcakes. It was to unite bakers to bake cupcakes that could then be distributed to homeless shelters, women's shelters and inner city youth programs.

Her hard work of campaigning to find both causes to donate to and people to do the baking and creating took off so well that the project ended up turning in 2000 Cupcakes; thousands of men, women and children were given a little taste of love around Christmastime that year.

These are the kinds of people who change the world.

## Martin and Peter

I heard the following story from a friend of mine named Arman. I'll let him tell it.

> *Several years ago I went to Guangzhou, China, to visit my father who was there being treated at a well-known hospital for cancer. When my father was diagnosed with pancreatic cancer, I relocated for a year to accompany my father while he through*

*treatments in Guangzhou.*

*It was there that I met two individuals from Europe named Martin and Peter.*

*I first met Martin. When I first saw him, I wondered to myself why this man looked so lonely.*

*I noticed he was all alone. He didn't have any guests or family with him. He would walk through the halls of the hospital all by himself.*

*Now just so you know, hospitals in China are different from hospitals here in North America.*
*If you go to a hospital in China, you pay for the room and the actual medical treatments you are receiving. For your daily meals, even as a patient, you need to be prepared to call out every time for catering services. If you have family there, your family can cook for you and bring the meals for you.*

*But Martin was alone.*

*I thought to myself how brave he was to come to this hospital alone with nobody to help take care of him. I always wondered what happened to him. What was his story?*
*So in my curiosity, I ended up talking to him and asking him about his situation.*

*What he told me broke my heart.*

*He had come from Scotland. He was recently diagnosed with stomach cancer which was very bad. He looked for doctors who could try to help him there, but to no avail. After months of tests and treatment, the doctors gave up and pronounced a death sentence over him.*

*But Martin was a fighter. Instead of giving up, he researched on the internet for possible solutions. After looking long and hard he found out that in China there was a very good cancer hospital that could take care of him and give him some hope. So he decided to come to Guangzhou.*

*Now before he left for China, his wife told him that she didn't want to take care of him anymore, that the burden was too much and the price was too high. She told him that because he was sick, he could not support her, could not give her joy and would end up ruining her life as she had to take care of him. Because she didn't want that kind of life, she was leaving him. Just like that, he lost his wife to divorce.*
*Martin came alone to China, with whatever money he had left and started to receive treatment in the hospital there.*
*As he was telling me his story, my heart broke for him. I told him I wish there was something I could do. He responded, "Don't worry Arman. Tomorrow my friend Peter will come."*

*"Oh really? You have friends who live in China?" I asked.*
*"No, my friend from Scotland."*
*"Really? Your friend is coming all the way from Scotland?"*
*I thought to myself, wow, Scotland is not exactly next door to China. It's about an eleven to twelve hour flight.*
*Is there really a friend who would be willing to travel that far just to visit another friend?*

*The next day, I did meet Martin's friend, Peter.*
*Through conversations I found out that Martin and Peter worked*

*for the same company, Scandinavian Airlines. Martin was a flight attendant and Peter was a senior captain pilot.*

*I also found out that Peter made a decision to move his family from Scotland to Hong Kong. He quit his job at Scandinavian Airlines and tried to find another job in Hong Kong as a pilot with Dragon Air. And he did just that. He moved his family to Hong Kong and landed a job with Dragon Air. He said he did that because with Dragon Air he would fly for two weeks and then have two weeks off.*

*He figured it was a good job for him because it allowed him to help take care of Martin. He could fly for two weeks and then for the other two weeks he could go to China by train (a one-hour trip) and help Martin during his stay at the hospital until he recovered.*
*I said to Peter, "Wow, you are an amazing man."*
*Peter's reply was, "Arman, I think you are a Christian right? Doesn't it say in the Bible that if you have a friend who has a need, that you are to help that friend in need?"*

*You know as a Christian, I felt like I was slapped in the face with the Word of God.*
*He continued, "I know you'd do the same thing, so what I am doing is nothing special."*
*I don't know if Peter is a Christian or not, but he sure taught me a lesson that day.*

*Peter was willing to leave his high paying job with a good Airline company, to work with a smaller airline, in a foreign land, for half the salary, and to move his whole family to a different country . . . just to help take care of and serve a friend.*

When I heard this story, I almost cried.

This was an example of "laying down your life for a friend." These are the kind of acts that God works through.

It's not so much the church services, or revival meetings or prayer meetings. Not to say any of those are wrong or not good. But true love always takes action.

Action without prejudice.
Action that doesn't discriminate.
Just people who *"ginosko"* God, and then lay down their lives for others.

My prayer for you today is that you first and foremost know and believe God's love for you. Then that you will turn around and bless the people around you with the same love.

It's through this simple formula that I believe the world can and will change for His glory.

The Lord bless you and keep you, the Lord make His face shine upon you and be gracious to you, the Lord lift up His countenance upon you and give you peace.

# Endnotes

**Chapter 1: You Ain't Seen Nothing Yet**

1. St Andrews Junior High School in Toronto

2. Johnsview Village Public School

3. Who are 'they' anyway?

4. Summer Retreat that changed my life was held at Jackson's Point Salvation Army Conference Centre. - http://www.sajpcc.com/

5. Pastor John Platinitus. Love that guy.

6. York Mills Collegiate Institute in Toronto

7. Mr. Patterson, grade 10 Geography teacher

8. Pastor Anthony Does

9. Mandy Mayhew

10. This is a true story and one I will never forget.

**Chapter 2: Then He Spoke**

11. Chris Ellie. I'll never forget your deep revelation about Nebuchadnezzar's vision of the statue

12. The NIV translates this "shall not" but some of the more

accurate translations including the original language show 'should not'.

## Chapter 3: What Have We Done with Jesus?

13. Luke 10:38-42

14. The Hour with George Stromboulopoulos - www.cbc.ca/strombo

15. A. J Jacobs, editor at large at Esquire magazine and author of three New Tork Times bestsellers. - www.ajjacobs.com

## Chapter 4: The Realities of Love

16. Flavius, Josephus and Betty Radice. The Jewish War. p. 1-111. Cambridge, Mass: Harvard Press. 1927.

17. Flavius, Josephus. Jewish Antiquities. Trans. H. St. J. Thackeray. Cambridge, Mass: Harvard Press. 1937.

18. Achtemeier, Paul. Harper's Bible Dictionary. p. 914. Harpercollins. 1985.

19. Davis, John D. Ed. Gehman, Henry Snider. Westminster Dictionary of the Bible. p. 538. Westminster Press. 1944.

20. Eastman, Mark. Dr. "Medical Aspects of the Crucifixion: The Agony of Love." Koinonia House. Khouse.org. 1998. Accessed 21 Apr. 2012. http://www.khouse.org/articles/1998/113/

## Chapter 5: Love?

21. First heard this "concept" of seeking the gift verses the giver from Tommy Tenny

## Chapter 6: The Real Definition of Love

22. The whole concept of the real definition of love was first introduced to me by Joseph Prince. A wonderful teacher on the Grace of God who ended up heavily influencing my life and ministry. Many of his concepts are shared throughout this chapter and the rest of this book.

23. Narayanan Krishnan was a CNN Hero - www.cnn.com/SPECIALS/cnn.heroes/archive10/naryanan.krishnan.html

24. For further reading on this idea, see Robert Capon's The Mystery Of Christ

## Chapter 7: Abba

25. I love kids, but they can be a little rambunctious sometimes.

26. I was first introduced to this 'Father Heart Of God teaching when I heard the late Jack Frost teach about it at a conference.

## Chapter 8: Distorted Father Images

27. Ed Piorek - The Father Loves You. Vineyard International Publish (1999)

**Chapter 9: Prodigal God**

28. The story of the "Prodigal Son" can be found in Luke 15:11-32

29. McClung Jr., Floyd. The Father Heart of God. Eugene: Harvest House Publishers. 1985.

**Chapter 10: Daddy Loves You**

30. Learned this through one of Joseph Prince's teaching.

31. The story of Abraham offering Isaac as an offering is found in Genesis 22:1-14

32. ~ Anslie P, 22 Mar. 2000. After receiving the Father's love during a service on the Father heart of God.

**Chapter 11: Knowing and Believing**

33. The story of David and Goliath can be found in 1 Samuel 17.

34. Missler, Chuck. "A Hidden Message: The Gospel in Genesis." Koinonia House. Khouse.org. 2012. Accessed 21 Apr. 2012. http://www.khouse.org/articles/1996/44/

35. Luke 10:29

**Chapter 12: What now?**

36. "Scott Harrison (charity founder)." Wikipedia.com Wikimedia Foundation. 10 Mar. 2012. Accessed 21 Apr. 2012. http://en.wikipedia.org/wiki/Scott_Harrison_(charity_founder)

37. "Scott's Story." Charity : water. Charitywater.org. 20 Mar. 2012. Accessed 21 Apr. 2012. http://www.charitywater.org/about/scotts_story.php

38. I heard these stories from Rob Bell's "The God's Aren't Angry" tour video.

39. This story was taken from Rob Bell's "Velvet Elvis". Zondervan Books; 1 edition (Jun 29 2006)

Nicholas Kusmich is also the founder and director of:

**The SOZO Commission**
www.sozocommission.com

A Ministry dedicated to bringing the fullness of God's salvation to the entire world through teaching, conferences, outreaches, publications.

**The EQUIP Academy**
www.equipacademy.com

An online learning platform designed to equip and empower you to live in the fullness of life and the fulfillment of your destiny.